A TIME TO
PLANT

Fifth Reader Teacher's Manual

I know that, whatsoever God doeth, it shall be for ever: nothing can be put to it, nor any thing taken from it: and God doeth it, that men should fear before him.

FROM ECCLESIASTES CHAPTER THREE

A TIME TO PLANT

Fifth Reader Teacher's Manual

Rod and Staff Publishers, Inc.
P.O. Box 3, Hwy. 172
Crockett, Kentucky 41413
Telephone (606) 522-4348

ISBN 978-07399-0403-9

Catalog no. 11592

5   6   7   8   9   —   24   23   22   21   20   19   18   17   16   15

TABLE OF CONTENTS

Tests

INTRODUCTION

Pupil's Workbook

Each lesson in the workbook begins with a paragraph that introduces the reading selection. These paragraphs are designed to give background information and focus the students' attention on the Biblical or moral theme of the lesson.

The workbook exercises are arranged in three parts.

Part A (Defining for Comprehension) contains vocabulary exercises such as matching words to definitions, filling in missing words, and defining from context. An occasional phonics exercise is included in this section.

Part B (Reading for Comprehension) consists of objective exercises that the average student should be able to complete on his own by carefully reading the lesson selection. This part includes questions about details in the selection, true-or-false exercises, sequencing exercises, and multiple-choice exercises.

Part C (Writing for Comprehension) contains subjective questions that students are to answer in complete sentences, or the exercises may deal with summarizing and outlining. The teacher will probably need to give extra help with this section, especially to slower students.

Some lessons also have Part D (Review), which provides review for the concepts taught in this course as well as for some vocabulary words. The tests are based on these reviews.

Note: The workbook is designed to accompany the 2005 edition of Grade 5 Reader. The 2005 edition contains numerous minor changes and an extensive revision of the two selections named below. However, the present workbook is intended to be compatible with all editions of the reader. If a difference in editions significantly affects the answer to a workbook exercise, the answer key has a note of explanation.

    22. Flat-tail: An Autumn Night in the Life of a Beaver

        (Formerly "Square-tail: An Autumn Day in the Life of a Beaver")

    37. Rebellion in the Hive

Tests

A separate test booklet contains tests that are to be given after every six lessons. Each test deals primarily with the material taught in the six preceding lessons, although there is some occasional overlap.

The lesson before each test has a review section designed as a study guide for the test. Be sure to remind students to do this review in preparation for the test. You may want to go over some of the points with them. Terms for literary concepts are highlighted where they are introduced so that students can easily find and review them. These terms are also reviewed in the review sections of other lessons.

Some tests begin with an exercise that tests the students' concentration. These exercises require the teacher to read a given passage orally to the students. Read these passages clearly, and make sure the students are paying attention and understand the directions.

Teacher's Manual

The teacher's edition contains the pupils' exercises with the answers filled in. The answers to subjective questions are not meant to be final, but rather to serve as a guide for evaluating the students' responses. Since complete sentence answers could be given in several forms, many answers include only the main points that a student is expected to have.

For each lesson, the teacher's edition contains a section entitled "To the Teacher." This section gives a few suggestions for teaching the lesson, but they are not exhaustive. It will finally be up to you to choose the approach that is most beneficial for your students.

During oral reading sessions—which should be held regularly—do not make the mistake of accepting or using substandard elocution. Appropriate emphasis and clear, correct enunciation are vital reading skills. Also, the printed page is not intended to be a race course; there is no merit in a student's reading speed outrunning his comprehension speed.

Make use of the discussion themes suggested in To the Teacher. Class discussions provide an excellent opportunity to develop and evaluate the listening and speaking skills of your students. Discussions should be conducted in an orderly fashion. The learning process is a disciplined process: Good speakers are disciplined speakers, and good listeners are disciplined listeners. During discussion periods, encourage your students to ask meaningful questions and to give meaningful responses to the questions you ask them.

Most lessons in the teacher's edition have a section of questions called "Discussion Starters." You may ask these questions along with the discussion themes suggested or use them independently. It is a good idea to ask questions regularly during the course of an oral reading session because they stimulate thinking and improve comprehension.

Checking Students' Work

The main thing to evaluate is comprehension; but things such as neatness, correct grammar, and clarity of expression should also carry some weight. If an otherwise correct answer can hardly be deciphered or is a grammatical disaster, full credit is not in order. After all, not only *what* we do is important but also *how* we do it.

As much as is practical, you should review your students' corrected work with them as soon as possible. The learning process is frustrated if students never find out whether an answer is right or wrong, or why an incorrect answer is wrong and what the right answer is.

Every twelfth lesson in this course is a composition lesson. The chart on page 9 may be used as an aid in scoring the compositions. The chart is divided into four areas of evaluation. Adding together the number of points for each item gives the total number of points for the composition.

View improved comprehension as the principal goal of this reading course. We may be able to speak words and hear words, and to write words and read words; but if we do not understand what the words mean, these mechanics will be of no value.

Scoring Chart for Compositions

1. Organization and Development

Composition sticks to the main idea.	10
Paragraphs are well developed with details, examples, and illustrations.	10
Progression of thought is orderly.	10
Opening is effective.	5
Conclusion is effective.	5

2. Vocabulary

Right words are used in the right way.	10
Original wording is used; trite expressions are avoided.	10

3. Sentence Structure

Sentences are grammatically complete.	6
Sentence parts are arranged well.	7
There is good variety in sentence types.	7

4. Spelling, Punctuation, Handwriting

Spelling is correct.	5
Capitalization is proper.	5
Punctuation is acceptable.	5
Handwriting is readable.	5
Total possible points	100

1. To Market

This story takes place in the Philippines. As you read it, notice how the lives of these children are different from yours. Also notice how these people used the blessings God gave them. Kindness is an important virtue to people of all lands.

A. Defining for Comprehension

The following words are found in the story in the order listed. Write the letter of the matching definition before each word.

c	1. wares	a.	Rough or unpleasant.
h	2. booths	b.	Confused mixture; jumble.
g	3. fare	c.	Goods or merchandise for sale.
f	4. landmarks	d.	Walkways between rows or counters.
d	5. aisles	e.	Convince; make someone believe.
i	6. bargained	f.	Buildings or other things that help people know where they are.
a	7. harsh		
j	8. linger	g.	Money charged for a ride.
b	9. medley	h.	Partly enclosed stalls for displaying merchandise.
e	10. persuade	i.	Tried to agree on a price.
		j.	Tarry; delay.

B. Reading for Comprehension

11. Mother had a long list of things for the children to buy. Why did she want them to go to the Quiapo market rather than to Pedring's store?

    The prices were higher at Pedring's. _____

    _____

12. People in the Philippines use jeepneys much as people in North America use **taxis (buses)**

13. In about the middle of the story, one sentence says, "Then Nenet stopped smiling for just a minute." What made her stop smiling?

    She thought about Angie and felt sorry for her. _____

    _____

14. What attracted the children to the pet shop? _____

    the harsh voices of parrots calling "Tuloy kayo" _____

5

Lesson 1

To the Teacher

Read the story to the class. Demonstrate the principles of proper reading: read clearly and distinctly, use proper voice inflection (such as at the ends of sentences), observe punctuation marks within sentences, practice good elocution, and so on. Remember that your students are looking to you as a model.

As you read the story, point out the footnotes that give the pronunciations of Quiapo (kē ä′ pō), Tuloy kayo (tŭ′ loi kī′ yō), and Salamat (sä lä′ mät). (Older editions of the reader do not have these footnotes.) Stop at convenient places to give explanations or to ask questions that will stimulate the students' thinking. For example, after reading the first paragraph,

point out the Philippine Islands and its capital, Manila, on a wall map.

Read on to where Mother told the children, "I'm sure you can go alone." Ask your students what Mother's decision indicated about her attitude toward the children. (She considered them dependable.)

Continue reading the next several paragraphs. Then ask your students what Nenet's comments about Angie tell them about Nenet. (She was kind and considerate.)

Discuss the Filipino custom of bargaining. Explain that bargaining for purchases is a common practice in many countries.

If you are alert, you will think of other questions or explanations that you can use to aid your students' comprehension of the story. Time spent in this way is not wasted. On

Fifth Reader Workbook

15. What animals, besides birds, did the children see in the pet shop?_____

___monkeys and fish_____

16. Here is a list of the main happenings in the story. Number them in the correct order.

    __2__ Nenet and Manuel waved to Angie as they waited for a jeepney.

    __4__ The children bought a pair of finches.

    __5__ Nenet and Manuel started for home.

    __1__ Mother gave the children permission to go to the market.

    __6__ The children decided to give the finches to Angie.

    __3__ Nenet and Manuel purchased the things on Mother's list.

17. The ***writer's purpose*** is the author's most important reason for writing a story. What is the writer's purpose in this story? Circle the letter of the best answer.

    a. To describe life in the Philippines.

    b. To show that a pet store is a good place to buy gifts for sick friends.

    c. To remind us to share our blessings with others.

    d. To show that by shopping carefully, it is possible to save money.

C. Writing for Comprehension

Write the answers in complete sentences.

18. What did winding streets that looked alike and crowds of people have to do with Mother's concern about the children going to market?

    __The children could easily get lost in the streets or among the crowds at the market.__

    _____

19. Read John 6:5–11. How were Nenet and Manuel like the lad in this Bible story?_____

    __They were willing to share the little they had with others.__

20. Read the last line in the story. In one or two sentences, explain why Nenet and Manuel's mother "looked even happier than before."

    __Their mother looked happier because she was more pleased with the children's__

    __kindness and generosity than she had been with their choice of a treat.__

    _____

6

the contrary, it may prove to be the most important element on your part in developing your students' understanding.

You may want to discuss Part C (Writing for Comprehension) with the students. Encourage them to think and to write well-worded answers according to the context of the story. You may want to give them a few hints, but have them formulate answers in their own words.

Literary concept in this lesson:

Writer's purpose (Discuss exercise 17 in class.)

Discussion Starters

1. How did Manuel signal the jeepney driver to stop? (by whistling)

2. What made the children bargain carefully? (Mother gave them permission to buy sweets or toys with the money that was left.)

3. What does *Tuloy kayo* mean? (Come in.)

4. What picture do you get of the monkeys when it says they were "scratching, chewing, and chattering"? (Answers will vary.)

5. What was Manuel and Nenet's mother like? (industrious, concerned for her children, generous, kind)

6. How do you know that the two children knew each other very well? (They knew each other's thoughts without speaking.)

2. The Second Mile

The writer's purpose in this story is to show how the way of love can draw people together and make friends out of enemies. Roman soldiers were taught to hate and kill their enemies, but here was a new and better way, one we should follow in our own lives.

A. Defining for Comprehension

1. a. Find the word **figure** in the third paragraph of the story. Is this word used as a noun or a verb in this sentence? <u>as a noun</u>

   b. Write a sentence of your own, using **figure** in the same way it is used in the story.
   <u>(Sample answer.) I watched the figure coming up the steps.</u>

2. a. The words **sullenly** and **bitter** are used to tell how David felt when he was ordered to carry the soldier's pack. Were his feelings loving or hateful? <u>hateful</u>

   b. Now write an antonym for **sullenly** and an antonym for **bitter.** (Sample answers given.)
   <u>cheerfully, happily</u>   <u>sweet, pleasant</u>

The following words are found in the story in the order listed. Write the letter of the matching definition before each word.

<u>h</u>	3. bulky	a.	Violation of rights; unfairness.
<u>f</u>	4. eased	b.	Lifted to the shoulder.
<u>e</u>	5. sullenly	c.	Walking with heavy steps.
<u>a</u>	6. injustice	d.	Held tightly.
<u>i</u>	7. bitter	e.	Gloomily and angrily.
<u>c</u>	8. plodding	f.	Placed slowly and carefully.
<u>j</u>	9. amazement	g.	Walked with long steps.
<u>b</u>	10. shouldered	h.	Heavy and clumsy.
<u>d</u>	11. clasped	i.	Resentful; hateful.
<u>g</u>	12. strode	j.	Great surprise.

Lesson 2

To the Teacher

Review the principles of good reading mentioned in Lesson 1. Then give the children an opportunity to read aloud to the class. Have them take turns reading the story by paragraphs. Commend them when they observe the qualities you discussed with them. Pupils will normally read louder and more clearly if they stand.

After reading the first several paragraphs, direct the students' attention to the sentence that says, "If it weren't for them [the Romans], we Jews would be free again!" Discuss the fact that the Jews were under Roman rule at the time of this story.

Continue reading to the point where David nearly runs into the Roman soldier. Discuss Jesus' ministry in light of these oppressive times. Why was it especially difficult for the Jews to accept the Sermon on the Mount while living under Roman rule? What type of rulers were the Romans? Do you think the one-mile law was harsh?

Literary concepts in this lesson:

Concentration (Discuss exercise 13 in class.)
Main idea (Discuss exercise 19 in class.)

Fifth Reader Workbook

B. Reading for Comprehension

13. To *concentrate* means to pay close attention to something. How well did you concentrate? The first paragraph of the story gives a picture of what David saw on the great road. Without looking back, underline the things in the list below that are mentioned in that paragraph. Then look at the paragraph and change any wrong answers.

     cars   <u>people</u>   cows   <u>donkeys</u>   <u>camels</u>   ox carts

14. Why did the Roman soldier not bother looking back to see if David was following?
    <u>He knew that David would not dare to disobey.</u>

15. Which verse in Matthew 5 tells us to go an extra mile if we are forced to go one mile?
    <u>verse 41</u>

16. Who was the Master and Teacher that David was thinking about? <u>Jesus</u>

17. At one point in the story, David asked himself, "Why should I go more than one mile?" If David had not remembered the Master's words, what would he probably have done after walking one mile? Circle the letter of the best answer.
    a. David would have offered to carry the soldier's pack two more miles.
    b. David would have rested and asked the soldier to share a meal with him.
    c. David would have thrown the pack on the ground and walked away.

18. What two things about the Roman soldier did David notice for the first time after offering to carry the pack farther than the law required?
    <u>David noticed that the soldier was young and that he was tired.</u>

19. The most important truth or lesson in a story is the *main idea* of the story. A three-word sentence spoken by the soldier near the end of the story gives the main idea. Write that sentence.
    <u>Love your enemies.</u>

C. Writing for Comprehension

20. How did the remembrance of the Master's teachings change David's feelings toward the Roman soldier?
    <u>It helped David to forget his bitterness toward the soldier and be a friend to him.</u>

8

Discussion Starters

1. Near the beginning of the story, why did David have angry thoughts about the soldier? (He was one of the Roman soldiers who kept the Jews from being free.)
2. How did the soldier know he had walked a mile? (The Roman mile was a thousand paces. There were milestones along many Roman roads.)
3. Why was the soldier surprised when David offered to go the second mile? (Most boys would have resented carrying the soldier's pack *one* mile.)
4. Was the second mile really a short one? Explain. (No. It seemed short because David and the soldier were having a good discussion.)

21. In one or two sentences, tell why you think the Roman soldier said, " 'Love your enemies.' That is a hard teaching." _____

   <u>__This was completely different from hating and killing enemies as he had been taught.__</u>

   _____

D. Review

22. Three new concepts are introduced in Lessons 1 and 2. They all appear in ***print like this.*** Write the meaning of each term.

   a. writer's purpose <u>__the author's most important reason for writing a story__</u>

   b. concentrate <u>__to pay close attention to something__</u>

   c. main idea <u>__the most important truth or lesson in a story__</u>

23. Write the meanings of these words from Lesson 1.

   a. fare <u>__money charged for a ride__</u>

   b. medley <u>__confused mixture; jumble__</u>

   c. persuade <u>__convince; make someone believe__</u>

Fifth Reader Workbook

 3. It's in Your Face

This poem describes our face as a barometer that shows how we live. A barometer is an instrument that measures changes in air pressure and indicates what kind of weather is coming. Likewise, the expressions on our face indicate what we are like and how we are living.

A. Defining for Comprehension

1. Underline the best answer: A barometer is most like a (hammer, <u>tape measure,</u> saw).

2. Sometimes we can tell what a new word means by the way it is used in a sentence. This is called *defining from context.* The first line of stanza 2 has the word **deceit.** Another word in the same line has nearly the same meaning and helps to explain the meaning of **deceit.** Write that word. <u>false</u>

3. Write the meaning of **sinew.** <u>tendon</u>

4. What word in the third stanza is a synonym for **boundless** or **eternal**? <u>infinite</u>

5. The first line of the third stanza contains the phrase "if for others you live." Write a word from this stanza that has the same idea. <u>unselfish</u>

B. Reading for Comprehension

6. Think about the line, " For sinew and blood are a thin veil of lace." By this the author is saying that the expressions on our face will not hide our inner feelings. Why do you think he chose the phrase "thin veil of lace"? Circle the letter of the best answer.

   a. A veil of lace is pretty, but it is hard to make.
   b. A veil of lace is pretty because of its complex design.
   c. A veil of lace is pretty, but people can easily see through it.

7. According to the poem, why do we not have to tell others that we are living close to God?
   <u>It will show in your face.</u>

C. Writing for Comprehension

8. If we are sad or troubled, it is not wise to hide our feelings from those who love us. Write a paragraph explaining why this is so. **(Sample points to be mentioned.)**

   <u>We should not try to hide worry or sadness from our parents, teachers, and older brothers and sisters, because they can help us. They want to know how we feel because they love us. The Bible teaches that we should be sincere and honest. If we do not get help, the problem will only become worse.</u>

10

Lesson 3

To the Teacher

This lesson should be done in class if possible. Approach it as a matter of interest rather than making students feel responsible for their hearts. Be sure to discuss exercise 8 before assigning it.

Allow the pupils a few minutes to read the poem silently. Then select a student to read the poem aloud, or read it aloud yourself, observing the principles of good oral reading.

Discuss the main teaching of how hard it is to hide our feelings. Ask the pupils if it is really honest for people to try to hide their feelings. If feelings or attitudes are not right, what can we do other than trying to hide them? (Discuss the matter with the person involved.)

Literary concept in this lesson:

Defining from context (Discuss exercise 2 in class.)

4. Conquering With Kindness

This story shows us how true nonresistance works. According to the Bible, the Christian is to show love rather than trying to get even when someone mistreats him. Sometimes this brings the offender to repentance.

A. Defining for Comprehension

1. Some of the words below describe Neighbor White, and some describe the shoemaker as he was at the beginning of the story. Write these words under the correct headings to show whom they describe.

		Neighbor White	**Shoemaker**
patient	considerate	patient	rude
rude	impatient	generous	selfish
selfish	polite	considerate	impatient
generous	harsh	polite	harsh

2. One sentence tells about a terrible squalling among the geese. What other word in that sentence suggests that **squalling** refers to a sound?   heard

3. Underline the correct answers.

   a. The children found the geese mangled and dead in the bushes. The meaning of **mangled** is (piled up, battered, smothered).

   b. The last syllable of **mischief** rhymes with (whiff, thief, life).

B. Reading for Comprehension

4. Here is a list of the main happenings in the story. Number them in the correct order.

   _3_ The shoemaker's hogs ate Neighbor White's corn.

   _1_ The shoemaker complained to Neighbor White about his geese.

   _6_ The shoemaker confessed that he had killed Neighbor White's geese.

   _4_ The shoemaker wanted to pay Neighbor White for the damage his hogs had done.

   _2_ The shoemaker killed Neighbor White's geese.

   _5_ Neighbor White refused to accept payment for his corn.

   _7_ The shoemaker and Neighbor White became good neighbors.

5. Copy a verse from Romans 12 that teaches doing good to conquer evil.

   "Be not overcome of evil, but overcome evil with good."(verse 21)

   (Verse 19 is also acceptable.)

11

Lesson 4

To the Teacher

After the students have read the story silently, have one of them read Romans 12:17–21 aloud. Discuss the story in light of this Scripture passage.

Be sure the students understand that "I" in the story is Neighbor White and that his neighbor is the shoemaker.

Encourage the students to note the differences in personalities between the shoemaker and Neighbor White. Guide them in evaluating personalities by explaining that character is revealed by how a person acts, what he says, how he says it, and how he responds to the words and actions of other people. Ask the pupils if such things had any effect on the shoemaker's manner of acting and reacting. Also discuss the character words in exercise 1.

This story is well suited to oral reading. Encourage the students to read with expression. The story could be read several times, with the parts of Neighbor White and the shoemaker assigned to different pairs of students. You may want to have the same pair read the story twice, with reversed roles in the second reading.

Discussion Starters

1. What could Neighbor White have done differently near the beginning of the story that would have solved everything? (He could have penned in the geese as his neighbor requested.)

Fifth Reader Workbook

6. Near the end of the story, the shoemaker told Neighbor White that he had something laboring on his mind. Carefully read the paragraph in which this phrase is found. Then circle the letter of the sentence below that best explains what the shoemaker meant.

 a. "I have a terrible headache."

 b. "My conscience is bothering me."

 c. "I am worried."

 d. "I have a difficult problem to solve."

7. The main idea of this story and "The Second Mile" are much the same. Circle the letter of the sentence below that best tells how the two main ideas are alike.

 a. They both show the blessings of willingly helping another person.

 b. They both describe an event that took place in the past.

 c. They both show how acts of kindness can draw people together.

8. Circle the letter of the phrase that tells what was conquered with kindness in this story.

 a. Neighbor White's geese

 b. the shoemaker's unneighborly feelings

 c. Neighbor White's kindness

 d. the shoemaker's hogs

C. Writing for Comprehension

9. What would probably have happened if Neighbor White had killed the shoemaker's hogs when he found them eating his corn? Answer in one or two sentences.   (Sample answers.)

 <u>They would have remained enemies.</u>

 <u>The shoemaker's attitude would not have changed.</u>

10. Write a paragraph explaining why it would have been wrong for Neighbor White to kill the shoemaker's hogs when he found them eating his corn.

 <u>(Paragraph should refer to Bible principles such as love and nonresistance. It could</u>

 <u>also mention points such as the hogs only doing what was natural for them and</u>

 <u>not being responsible for the hostility involved.)</u>

2. Neighbor White told his children, "All keep still, and let us deal in kindness." What would have happened if he had said, "How terrible! Let's put him in his place"? (A serious quarrel would probably have started.)

3. What do you suppose Neighbor White expected from the shoemaker the next time he met him? (He probably expected more angry words from the shoemaker, such as, "I told you I'd take care of your geese, and I did!")

4. Does kindness always conquer? (In normal circumstances it usually does. But sometimes no amount of kindness will make any difference, such as at the crucifixion of Jesus or the stoning of Stephen.)

D. Review

Write whether each sentence is true (**T**) or false (**F**).

___T___ 11. The word **figure** can be used as a noun.

___F___ 12. The main idea of a story is the author's most important reason for writing the story.

___T___ 13. A barometer measures changes in air pressure.

Fifth Reader Workbook

 5. The Hunters

The Lord provides in various ways for our physical well-being. Many of us are familiar with gardening or farming as a way of providing food. In this story you will meet people who depended largely on hunting to provide food because gardening in the cold northland is not practical. As you might enjoy growing some fresh vegetables in a garden of your own, so the Inuit boys in this story were eager to help provide food for their people by hunting.

A. Defining for Comprehension

Write the letter of the matching definition before each word.

c	1. heather		a.	Draw a hook and line through water.
b	2. tundra		b.	Treeless plain of the Arctic region.
d	3. disc		c.	Small flowering evergreen shrub.
h	4. somber		d.	Circular form or shape.
g	5. glistening		e.	Artificial bait used for fishing.
i	6. squalls		f.	Destroyed; ruined.
f	7. dashed		g.	Sparkling.
a	8. troll		h.	Dull or dark; gloomy.
e	9. lure		i.	Sudden violent winds with rain or snow.
k	10. resumed		j.	Ate greedily.
m	11. fragile		k.	Began again; went back to.
n	12. thong		l.	Without slackening; persistent.
r	13. agony		m.	Delicate; easily broken.
j	14. gorged		n.	Leather lace or strip; strap.
q	15. eerie		o.	Fierceness; savageness.
p	16. gait		p.	Manner of walking or running.
l	17. relentless		q.	Weird; unnatural; frightening.
o	18. ferocity		r.	Intense pain; anguish.

14

Lesson 5

To the Teacher

Before you have the students read this story orally, tell them the correct pronunciations of the following words.

Avik (ā′ vĭk) Omak (ō′ măk) kayak (kī′ ăk)

inyukhuit (ĭn′ yək hüt) tuki (tü′ kē)

The setting of this story is so unique that the teacher will need to be involved quite directly. Show the location of Coronation Gulf on a map. It lies in the far north, between mainland Canada and Victoria Island.

People of the far north were formerly called Eskimos, but they object to that name because it means "eaters of raw meat." The accepted name is Inuit, which simply means "people" and is used by the Inuit themselves

As the students read the story aloud, help them to understand the significance of what they are reading. One thing that you can discuss is the peculiarities of the Arctic summer, as indicated in this sentence: "The red disc of the sun now touched the tips of the farthest hills at midnight." Ask, "Did the story take place at the beginning or toward the end of summer?" (Note that the wildflowers would soon be fading and the land would become brown and somber. This indicates that it was toward the end of summer.)

Discuss the blending of the past with the present. The boys had lost their rifles when their canoe was wrecked. On the other hand, they used a fishing lure carved of bone. Also

B. Reading for Comprehension

19. The *setting* of a story is the place and time in which it occurs. The setting of "The Second Mile" is Palestine while Jesus was on earth. Find three words or phrases that tell where today's story took place, and three words or phrases that tell when it took place. Write them under the correct headings.   (Other answers may also be correct.)

Where?	What season or time of day?
Coronation Gulf	evening sun
Arctic	summer
inland lakes	heat of day

20. Why did the boys set up a tent? __to keep off the mosquitoes__

21. Why had the boys not gone along with the rest of the caribou hunters?_____
    __They had wrecked their canoe and lost their rifles.__

22. What signal did Avik use to tell that he had spotted some game?_____
    __He bobbed up and down and threw up his arms.__

23. An *illustration* is a picture or diagram that makes writing clearer by helping the reader to "see" something. One illustration is the drawing of a jeepney in Lesson 1.

    With help from the story and a dictionary, draw a simple illustration of a kayak in the space below.   (Sample illustration.)

15

discuss how the boys made the best of a bad situation. Ask the students how learning from others helped the boys to succeed.

Seek to curb the hunting spirit that this story may stir up. Point out that for the Eskimos, hunting was not something to do for fun, but it was a necessary part of their struggle for existence. In the harsh climate of the Arctic, the difference between success and failure in hunting meant the difference between surviving and starving.

Discuss some of the words in Part A together. Suggested words to discuss orally: tundra, glistening, squalls, gait, ferocity.

Literary concepts in this lesson:

Setting (Discuss exercise 19 in class.)
Illustration (Discuss exercises 23 in class.)

Discussion Starters

1. What makes you think Avik and Omak were responsible boys? (They were disappointed at not being able to help with the caribou hunt. When Avik sighted game, the boys devised a way to get it.)
2. Did they live in fairly modern times? How do you know? (Yes. They had rifles, matches, and hunting knives.)
3. How did they keep mosquitoes out of the tent? (Avik set a match to some moss inside the tent.)
4. Discuss kayaks. Why did Avik need to steady it when Omak got in? (A kayak is a small boat covered with skins, which the user ties around his waist to keep water out. The kayak had to be steadied to keep it from

Fifth Reader Workbook

Write whether each sentence is true (**T**) or false (**F**).

   _T_   24. The boys had actually set out on this trip to catch fish.

   _F_   25. The caribou were frightened by a wolf.

   _T_   26. The inyukhuit were piles of stone.

   _T_   27. The boys cut the dead caribou open before they skinned them. (They ate raw liver.)

C. Writing for Comprehension

28. How did the inyukhuit help the boys catch the caribou?

    These piles of stone frightened the caribou and made them go in the right direction.

29. Explain why Omak forgot the agony of the mosquitoes when the caribou plunged into the lake.

    He was so excited about the hunt that he no longer noticed the discomfort caused by the mosquitoes.

16

tipping while someone was getting in.)

5. Did Omak ever fall out of his kayak? (No. The covering of skins tied around his waist kept him from falling out.)

6. Do you think the boys were proud of their hunting success? (Not necessarily. They were obviously pleased with their success, and rightly so.)

6. Which Are You?

This poem uses builders and wreckers to teach a lesson about people's lives. God wants His people to be builders for eternity. By living for God and others, we can be useful builders. On the other hand, if we live selfishly, we will be like wreckers who are out to destroy.

A. Defining for Comprehension

1. What word in the first stanza names a group of men working together? <u>gang</u>

2. What word names the one in charge of the group of workers? <u>foreman</u>

3. a. Which word in stanza 2 means "the parts that a person plays in life"? <u>roles</u>

   b. Write the homonym of this word, which describes the action of a ball. <u>rolls</u>

   c. Which of these words fits in the sentence below? <u>roles</u>

      While Mother was in the hospital, my big sister had the ___ of being cook and babysitter.

4. A square is a carpenter's tool. Copy the definition from your dictionary that fits the way it is used in the poem. <u>(Sample definition.)</u>
   <u>A tool used by builders for testing right angles.</u>

B. Reading for Comprehension

5. What is the message of the first stanza in this poem? Circle the letter of the best answer.

   a. Common labor is all we need.

   b. It is wrong to be a wrecking contractor.

   (c) It takes more effort to build than to wreck.

   d. We should be content with the labor of tearing down.

6. In stanza 2, lines 3–5 say that a builder uses a rule, a square, and a well-made plan. What is the rule, square, and plan that Christians use to build their lives? <u>the Bible</u>

7. In the second stanza of this poem, the author gives four descriptions of a builder. The sentence below gives the first of these. Write sentences that give the other three descriptions of a builder. Begin each sentence with a "A builder is a person who . . ."

   a. <u>A builder is a person who works with care.</u>

   b. <u>A builder is a person who measures life by rule and square.</u>

   c. <u>A builder is a person who shapes his deeds to a well-made plan.</u>

   d. <u>A builder is a person who patiently does the best he can.</u>

Lesson 6

To the Teacher

Be sure the pupils understand that the purpose of this poem is not to compare wrecking contractors with building contractors. Rather, it is talking about patterns of life.

The lesson can apply to the natural world. Ask the pupils who is the most careful and patient builder they have known. Perhaps a watchmaker or seamstress will come to their minds. Can they name a Bible character who is noted for his carefulness and diligence in building? (Noah, Genesis 6:22; Bezaleel, Exodus 38:22; 39:43; Nehemiah and his workers, Nehemiah 4:21–23)

Lead the pupils' considerations from the natural to the spiritual. Ask them, "What can a constructive person build up besides buildings?" They will probably be able to think of someone who often has a cheery word of encouragement, or who is noted for helping others.

Now help the pupils to see that this is really what the poem is talking about. Ask the pupils what phrases they can find in the poem that would confirm that the writer is talking about attitudes toward life ("measuring life," "shaping my deeds," "patiently doing the best," "walks the town").

Fifth Reader Workbook

C. Writing for Comprehension

8. How could you be a "wrecker" at school?_____

   __(Individual answers.)_____

   _____

9. Write a paragraph telling how you could build a friendship with a classmate.

   __(Individual answers.)_____

   _____

   _____

   _____

   _____

D. Review for Test 1

10. Be sure you know the meanings of the vocabulary words in Lessons 1–6.

11. Be sure you know what these terms mean.

    writer's purpose (Lesson 1)
    concentrate (Lesson 2)
    main idea (Lesson 2)
    defining from context (Lesson 3)
    setting (Lesson 5)
    illustration (Lesson 5)

(Tell students to use this review, as well as later reviews of this kind, to prepare for the tests that follow them.)

18

Discussion Starters

1. Which line suggests that the wreckers were doing their work in a fast, rough manner? ("With a ho-heave-ho and a lusty yell")
2. Why does it take more time and skill to build than to tear down? (Building requires planning and careful arrangement. Tearing down can be done with much less thought and preparation.)

7. A Sweet Story

The honeybee is a very interesting part of God's creation. As we learn about its development, we can be assured that only an all-wise God could have made something so marvelous.

A. Defining for Comprehension

Write the letter of the matching definition before each word.

  e   1. transparent   a. Came out.

  c   2. resembled   b. Comforting; pleasing.

  h   3. spurted   c. Looked like.

  d   4. reckons   d. Counts or calculates.

  j   5. effectiveness   e. Clear; able to be seen through.

  a   6. emerged   f. Dependable; trustworthy.

  g   7. completion   g. State of being finished.

  k   8. enclosure   h. Squirted out; gushed forth.

  b   9. soothing   i. Not pretty; unattractive.

  i   10. homely   j. Helpfulness; usefulness.

  f   11. reliable   k. Space surrounded by a fence or wall.

12. Find the sentence that says Baby Bee was called a larva after she came out of the egg. Then find another word nearby that is used instead of **larva**, and write it here.

   grub

B. Reading for Comprehension

13. The four stages in the life of a bee are adult, larva, egg, and pupa. Write these words in the order of a bee's life in the long blanks below. In the blank before a letter, write the number of the thing that happened in that growing stage.

   2   a.   egg   (1) Baby Bee gained a thousand times her weight in one week.

   1   b.   larva   (2) Baby Bee was glued to the floor of her cell.

   4   c.   pupa   (3) Baby Bee ate honey.

   3   d.   adult   (4) Baby Bee became colored.

Lesson 7

To the Teacher

As you have the pupils read this story orally, discuss with them the various stages of a bee's development. Have them read about the development of a bee during the time in which it is an egg, then discuss this with them. Next is the larval stage, which is covered further on. "Baby Bee Grows Up" begins with the pupa stage and continues into the adult stage. You could increase your students' interest and understanding by drawing on the blackboard an illustration of each stage of the bee's development as you read about it. Be sure to reflect the growing size of each stage.

Point out the many comparisons that are used in this story to help us better understand the development of a bee. Some comparisons are literal, such as "in the shape of a sausage" and "weighing as much as a large farm tractor." Others are figurative: "like a light bulb in a socket" and "a delicate little sleeping bag." Comparisons are useful because they help us to understand something unknown by relating it to something known.

A figure of speech is a special, imaginative comparison between two things that are not really similar. However, fifth graders are hardly able to comprehend fully how a figurative comparison differs from a literal one, so keep your explanation brief and simple. Make it clear that a simile is a figure of speech with a word such as *like* or *as*. A metaphor omits these words and makes a statement that is true only in the figurative

Fifth Reader Workbook

14. Writers often use comparisons called *figures of speech* to give a clearer picture of what they describe. One common figure of speech is the *simile* (sĭm′ ə lē). A simile compares by saying that something is **like** or **as** another thing. Here is an example from the story: "like a light bulb in a socket."

   Another common figure of speech is the *metaphor* (mĕt′ ə fôr). A metaphor compares by saying that one thing **is** or **was** another thing. Here is an example from the story: "a very homely and unattractive sausage it was." A metaphor may also say that something happens which is true only in a figurative way. Here is a Bible example: "The mountains skipped like rams, and the little hills like lambs" (Psalm 114:4).

   Write whether each phrase below contains a simile (**S**) or a metaphor (**M**).

   __S__ a. food as sour as vinegar and as hot as red pepper

   __S__ b. was shaped like a banana

   __M__ c. a delicate little sleeping bag of fine web

   __M__ d. the little sausage divided itself

15. Write whether each sentence is true (**T**) or false (**F**).

   __F__ a. Bees can work as soon as they come out of the cell.

   __F__ b. Bees live to be forty years old.

   __F__ c. Royal jelly tastes like condensed milk.

   __T__ d. Baby bees do not look at all like their parents at first.

C. Writing for Comprehension

16. What did the bee egg do a few hours before it hatched?
   It lay down on its side.

17. What is the job of the bee nurse?
   feeding royal jelly and closing off the cell after the grub is big enough

18. How did Baby Bee get out of her sealed wax cell?
   by scraping with her new legs and biting with her jaws

19. What jobs did Baby Bee do as soon as she was a week old?
   dusting the hive, making wax, building combs, being a nurse

20

sense. Simile: "They were as sheep not having a shepherd." Metaphor: "I am the good shepherd."

Some comparisons are borderline. Is "shaped like a banana" literal or figurative? Because that distinction is not emphasized, some comparisons that could be called literal are labeled similes in this book.

When a vocabulary list includes more than five words, be sure to discuss at least a few with the students. Include parts of speech in your discussion.

Literary concepts in this lesson:

Figures of speech, similes, and metaphors (Discuss exercise 14 in class. Challenge the students to find similes and metaphors as they read the story.)

Discussion Starters

1. How do you know that Baby Bee's eggshell was not like a hen's eggshell? (It was transparent. Baby Bee tore through the shell rather than breaking it.)
2. Why does Mother Bee put a dab of glue on each egg? (to hold the egg to the floor of its cell)
3. What color is ivory? (yellowish white, like an elephant's tusk)
4. In what ways did Baby Bee differ from human babies? (As a larva, she gained over a thousand times her weight in one week and changed her skin several times. She did various kinds of work around the hive when she was only a week old.)

8. James Dulin's Bargain

Covetousness is a great evil. This story shows clearly what can happen if a person becomes absorbed with the love of money.

A. Defining for Comprehension

Find each of the following words in the story and study its context to understand its meaning. Then without using a dictionary, write the letter of the matching definition before each word.

_e_	1. hoax	a. That on which something is built.
_g_	2. mother lode	b. A sample of something.
_c_	3. enthusiastic	c. Showing eagerness and excitement.
_b_	4. specimen	d. Great wealth.
_d_	5. fortune	e. Something used to deceive; a trick.
_a_	6. foundation	f. Provoked; irritated.
_f_	7. vexed	g. Rich vein of gold.
_m_	8. shame	h. Desirous; determined.
_k_	9. brooded	i. Use (property) as security to guarantee payment.
_j_	10. assayer	j. Person who tests ore.
_i_	11. mortgage	k. Thought moodily.
_n_	12. poverty	l. Plan in a sly way; plot.
_h_	13. intent	m. Distress caused by guilt.
_l_	14. scheme	n. The state of being poor.

15. The last line of the story tells us that James had become "obsessed" with riches. To help you understand the story better, find **obsess** in the dictionary and write its definition.

    to intensely or abnormally occupy the mind of

    Also write a definition for **covetous**.   a wrong desire for another person's possessions

B. Reading for Comprehension

16. What is one detail which indicates that the story took place at least a hundred years ago?

    (Sample answers.) Mr. Shillebah was riding a horse.

    People were going to California to seek gold (apparently in the 1849 gold rush).

21

Lesson 8

To the Teacher

Before having the students read this story, ask them if they have ever wanted anything very badly. Do they wish they were rich or that they had an easier life? Ask them if there is anything wrong with daydreaming about such things. Mention that they are about to read a story which illustrates one danger of desiring to be rich.

Discuss the meaning of *obsess*. Then as the pupils read the story, direct them to note how James becomes more obsessed with the desire for riches as the story develops. Also have them observe how this obsession causes him to act. If you have time, you could have them stop reading at convenient points and discuss the growing obsession together. Point out that James should have had the "gold" tested *before* buying the land, but apparently he was blinded by his obsession.

When the pupils have finished reading the story, ask them whether it was easy for James to see that he had been obsessed by a desire for gold. Help them to see that gold or money is not evil in itself, but that a desire for riches is wrong. (See Discussion Starters, number 4.)

You may want to discuss exercise 22 in class before assigning Part C.

Literary concept in this lesson:

Order of events (See exercise 18.)

Fifth Reader Workbook

17. Gold was discovered at Newburyport, Massachusetts, but James Dulin lived in the state of
    __New Hampshire__

18. The *order of events* is the order in which things happen in a story. Number the following sentences in the correct order.

    __4__ a. James first became provoked with his wife.

    __2__ b. James said New Hampshire was as likely to have gold as Massachusetts.

    __8__ c. James shouted at his wife and accused her of preaching.

    __1__ d. James found it hard to believe that gold had been found in Newburyport.

    __3__ e. James walked past his cottage without seeing it.

    __7__ f. James made a dishonest bargain with Mr. Shillebah.

    __5__ g. James became dissatisfied with earning a living the old way and began thinking his house was too small.

    __6__ h. James schemed about a way to possess the gold on Mr. Shillebah's land.

19. Where in the story can we first see that James had become obsessed with riches? Answer by copying one event from number 18 above. _____
    __James walked past his cottage without seeing it.__

20. Circle the letter of the Bible verse that best matches the main idea of this story.
    a. "Will he esteem thy riches? no, not gold, nor all the forces of strength" (Job 36:19).
    b. "There is a sore evil which I have seen under the sun, namely, riches kept for the owners thereof to their hurt" (Ecclesiastes 5:13).
    (c.) "For the love of money is the root of all evil: which while some coveted after, they have erred from the faith, and pierced themselves through with many sorrows (1 Timothy 6:10).

C. Writing for Comprehension

21. Explain what is meant by "ill-gotten riches." _____
    __riches gotten in a wrong way__

22

Discussion Starters

1. How do you know that James was usually a cheerful person? (At the beginning of the story, James answered his neighbor cheerily. Near the end of the story, he thought of the contented, happy state that he had lost through his greed and dishonesty.)

2. How did James discover the glittering substance? (He was trying to dig a woodchuck out of its hole.)

3. Is it wrong to be rich? (It is not riches, but the desire for riches that is wrong. Likewise, it is not having money, but loving money that is wrong.)

4. If James had really found gold, how might the story have ended? (James would probably have become very rich. But there would also have been many problems, including discord in his home, conflict with his neighbor, and crowds of people flocking in to seek gold.)

5. How do you know that Nancy was a good wife? (She could have harshly accused James because he lost their farm. Instead, she became his comforter and willingly accepted the poverty resulting from his foolish actions.)

22. Why was James Dulin's bargain a poor bargain? List as many reasons as you can think of.

___(Sample reasons.)___

___It was dishonest. It was brought about by greed.___

___It caused ill feelings and sadness in his home.___

___It resulted in the loss of his farm.___

D. Review

23. Two common figures of speech are the ___simile___ and the ___metaphor___ .

24. Which kind of figure of speech is in the sentence below? ___simile___

The surface of the lake was like a mirror.

23

Fifth Reader Workbook

 ## 9. The Daisy

This poem uses word pictures to help us catch a glimpse of God's greatness in creation. As we look at the marvels of nature about us, our hearts should be lifted in adoration to God, who made them all.

A. Defining for Comprehension

As a help to understand this poem, find words that have the meanings given in the underlined phrases below. Use your dictionary if you need it.

Stanza 1

1. A whole bank of flowers might look like <u>an army marching together.</u>   phalanx

Stanza 2

2. The starry night sky <u>curved</u> above our heads. _____   arched

3. The travelers eagerly awaited the <u>dawn's</u> first light. _____   dayspring's

4. The little green shoot will <u>lift up</u> its head when spring comes. _____   rear

Stanza 3

5. The pillow was <u>trimmed with short strings around the edges.</u> _____   fringed

6. The boy was thin, but his legs were <u>lean and strong.</u> _____   wiry

7. The plate was <u>made with a raised gold design</u> around its edge. _____   gold-embossed

Stanza 4

8. The child wept with tears that were <u>not kept back.</u> _____   unrestrained

9. This paper has the <u>official mark</u> of the government. _____   stamp

10. Consider the word **arched** in the second stanza. Then circle the letter of the statement below that best explains the meaning of "He that arched the skies."

   a. He that built the skies above the earth.

   (b.) He that formed the skies into a curve.

   c. He that made the stars move in a circular path.

11. Study the first two lines of stanza 2. Then circle the letter of the phrase below that best tells what is meant by "pours the dayspring's living flood."

   a. Pours rain on the earth, which causes floods.

   b. Causes the springs to rise and feed the rivers.

   (c.) Causes the sun to rise and flood the earth with light.

24

Lesson 9

To the Teacher

This poem is filled with beautiful imagery. Take time to help the students recognize it and develop an understanding of its meaning.

Encourage the students to think of God, who formed the heavens and poured forth the light, as using that light to reach down and draw forth a tiny bud from the earth. Then have them see God as molding the daisy's green cup and wiry stem, spinning its silver fringe of leaves, setting its golden center, and finally scattering daisies over hill, valley, and desert.

If possible, show the class a real daisy or a picture of one.

Discussion Starters

1. When God made daisies, was He thinking about How do you know? (Yes. God made daisies—and marvels of creation—so that we can see His gr and power.)

2. What are some other things in the creation th make us think about God? (Answers will vary.)

B. Reading for Comprehension

12. Circle the letter of the statement below that best tells what the first stanza of this poem means.

    a. We do not need to rely on armies to prove that God is near.

    b. We do not need anything but daisies to teach us about God.

    (c.) We do not need to study all the marvels of creation to know that God is near.

13. List three colors that the poet named in describing the daisy. _____

    __purple, gold, silver (Green is mentioned in older editions of the reader.)__

14. Which stanza suggests how God designed the daisy? __stanza 3__

15. The poem names three places where God scattered daisies. List those places.

    __hill, dale, desert__

C. Writing for Comprehension

16. In a sentence or two, explain what the last two lines of the poem mean. _____

    __Wherever man goes, he can see evidence of God.__

D. Review

17. Similes and metaphors are two common kinds of __figures of speech.__   .

18. Does the sentence below contain a simile or a metaphor? __metaphor__
    The still surface of the lake was a mirror.

19. Write whether each sentence is true (**T**) or false (**F**).

    __T__   a. To scheme means to plan in a sly way.

    __F__   b. A person who is enthusiastic is bored and lazy.

    __T__   c. A hoax is a trick.

Fifth Reader Workbook

 # 10. The Sacrifice

The word **sacrifice** in the title suggests that something valuable was given up for a good cause. In this story, the loss of a pet helped to change a man's attitude. Can we cheerfully give up a prized possession for the good of another person?

A. Defining for Comprehension

The following words are found in Part I of the story. With help from the context and a dictionary, write them in the correct blanks after the sentences below.

elated	apprehensively	retaliate
gingerly	accomplished	guidance
assured	agitatedly	carcass
stalked		

1. The angry man ___ out the door. _____ stalked _____

2. We looked ___ at the storm clouds in the sky. _____ apprehensively _____

3. Jesus taught us not to ___ when someone does evil to us. ____ retaliate ____

4. The neighbor yelled ___ at the cows in his cornfield. _____ agitatedly _____

5. Arlene ___ picked up the dead mouse. _____ gingerly _____

6. The hunter dragged the ___ of the deer to his truck. _____ carcass _____

7. We were ___ when the teacher announced on a nature hike. ____ elated ____

8. The Bible gives us ___ for our lives. _____ guidance _____

9. Mother ___ me that my sickness was not serious. _____ assured _____

10. We will not ___ much work while we are grumbling. _____ accomplish _____

Study the way these words are used in the story. Then without using a dictionary, write the letter of the matching definition before each word.

_f_	11. communication	a.	Unwilling; hesitant.
_d_	12. hastily	b.	Cutting off dead branches.
_e_	13. lame	c.	Walking leisurely; strolling.
_a_	14. reluctant	d.	Quickly and thoughtlessly; rashly.
_b_	15. pruning	e.	Crippled; disabled.
_c_	16. ambling	f.	Exchange of ideas; discussion.

26

Lesson 10

To the Teacher

Before you have your pupils read this story, ask them what some of their favorite pets or animals have been. Ask them if they have had trouble keeping their pets or animals where they should be. Have they had problems with things such as housing or feeding their pets? (See Discussion Starters, number 1.)

After reading Part I together, discuss reactions to unkind things that others have done to us. Is it right to get angry, to become upset, or to have ill feelings?

This story emphasizes how Mr. Whitney's attitude changed as a result of the Morelys' loving response to him,

even after he shot Ralph's calf. After reading the entire story, discuss the Morelys' response in light of Romans 12:17–21. Encourage the pupils to share with the class occasions when they or someone they know has returned good for evil and thereby softened another person's attitude.

You may want to discuss exercise 27 in class before assigning it.

Discussion Starters

1. Do you have a pet or a favorite animal? Has it ever been hard to keep the animal where it belongs? (Answers will vary.)

2. Why did Father think they should repair the fence? (He said they would not have Molly for long if they did not

17. Under the correct headings, write the words from the list below that describe Ralph's father and the words that describe Mr. Whitney as he was at the beginning of the story.

		Ralph's father	Mr. Whitney
hasty	unhappy	patient	hasty
patient	companionable	considerate	selfish
considerate	irritable	companionable	unhappy
selfish	understanding	understanding	irritable

B. Reading for Comprehension

How well did you concentrate? Without looking back at the story, underline the correct words to complete the sentences below. If you must look back for an answer, write **X** *before that sentence.*

18. As the story opens, Ralph and his father are mending the fence one morning in (March, June, September).

19. Ralph was (ten, twelve, fourteen) years old.

20. When Mr. Whitney shot Molly, she was in his (garden, raspberry patch, corn field).

21. Ralph's father (sold, butchered, buried) Molly's carcass.

22. Mr. Whitney (accepted, refused to accept) money for the damage Molly had caused.

23. The name of Ralph's second calf was (Molly Two, Molly, Molly Too).

C. Writing for Comprehension

24. Write at least three things that happened after Molly's death which show that Mr. Whitney's attitude had changed.   (Any three.)

     Mr. Whitney apologized for shooting Molly.

     He asked Ralph to chop wood for him. He offered Ralph hot chocolate.

     He paid Ralph extra well (and told him to buy another calf). He commented on Molly Too.

25. Which story that you studied earlier in this book has a main idea very similar to the one in this story?   Conquering With Kindness

26. Explain the meaning of today's story title.   Ralph's calf was the sacrifice that helped

     Mr. Whitney to become a more friendly neighbor.

27

repair the fence.)

3. How do you know that Ralph really liked his calf? (Ralph became upset when Mr. Whitney threatened to shoot Molly. He spent most of his spare time with his calf. He was very sad when Molly was killed.)

4. What is a sacrifice? (something valuable that is given up for a good cause)

5. Why do you think Mr. Whitney never actually said "I'm sorry"? (Saying "I'm sorry" was probably too humiliating for a man like Mr. Whitney.)

27. Write a paragraph to tell what might have happened if Ralph's father had called the police when the calf was shot.

   (Paragraphs are individual work but should contain appropriate ideas.)

   _____

   _____

   _____

   _____

11. Wanderers of the Sea

This composition is not a story but an essay. Rather than teaching a lesson through events that happened to someone, it describes icebergs and the dangers they present.

A. Defining for Comprehension

The following words are found in the essay. Write the correct ones in the blanks after the sentences below. You will not use all the words.

avoid	eventually	reflect
immense	mass	constantly
imperceptibly	brilliant	growlers
seaward	entirely	hoarse

1. We had to wait several weeks, but ___ the package arrived. __eventually__

2. John slammed on the brakes to ___ hitting the deer. __avoid__

3. God is ___ watching over us. __constantly__

4. If something changes ___, the change is barely noticeable. __imperceptibly__

5. An ___ rock is a very large rock. __immense__

6. Snow may ___ so much sunlight that it hurts our eyes. __reflect__

7. Brian looked ___ just in time to see the great whale surface. __seaward__

8. A sore throat can cause a ___ voice. __hoarse__

9. The sun is so ___ that you should not look directly at it. __brilliant__

10. An object is said to have great ___ if it is very large. __mass__

B. Reading for Comprehension

11. Here are some questions to see how well you concentrated. Try to answer them without looking back at the essay. If you must look back for an answer, write **X** before that question.

   a. In which season do icebergs begin moving southward? __in spring__

   b. Where do most icebergs have their birth? __Greenland__

   c. What fraction of an iceberg shows above the surface of the water? __one-eighth__

   d. Icebergs are never found more than four hundred miles south of a certain Canadian island. What island is this? __Newfoundland__

Lesson 11

To the Teacher

The story of the *Titanic* would add interest to this lesson. You may want to read the account on page 36 to the class.

The English word *iceberg* is a partial translation of the Dutch word *ijsberg,* which is pronounced almost the same and means "ice mountain."

This essay presents a good opportunity to do some map work with the class. Beginning at Greenland, trace the course of icebergs. Locate Newfoundland on the map, and a point about four hundred miles south of Newfoundland where the icebergs disappear.

Many children will not understand what an iceberg looks like in the water. The following examples could be drawn on the board for illustration.

Fifth Reader Workbook

12. Why is "Wanderers of the Sea" a good title for this essay? Circle the letter of the best answer.

   a. It describes how icebergs drift with the ocean currents, in no fixed route.

   b. It suggests that icebergs are a wonder of God's creation.

   c. It makes the reader think that the essay is about sailors.

13. According to the essay, when are icebergs most dangerous? _____

   __when they melt faster below the surface than above and can overturn quickly__

14. a. Copy a phrase with a simile that describes a loud sound. _____

   __a roar (or an explosion) like thunder__

   b. Copy a simile that describes the appearance of icebergs. _____

   __like beautiful castles__

15. In the second paragraph, icebergs are called immense floating islands. This figure of speech is a (simile, <u>metaphor</u>).

16. Find the paragraph that describes the various colors of icebergs. List all the colors mentioned.

   __pale green, brilliant blue, deep purple, gold, rose, white__

17. There are three main forms of composition, or writing. As mentioned in the introductory paragraph, "Wanderers of the Sea" is an ***essay.*** This is a composition that presents facts or opinions about a subject, usually without characters (people) as in a story.

   A ***story*** is a composition that teaches a lesson by telling about an event in the life of one or more characters. Most of the compositions in this reader are short stories.

   A ***poem*** is a kind of composition known for its rhyme and rhythm. Poems often use colorful expressions and figures of speech, and they are written in stanzas rather than paragraphs.

   a. If you should be asked to write several paragraphs about how clouds are formed, would you write a story or an essay? __essay__

   b. If you wanted to teach a lesson about honesty by writing about something that happened to someone, would you write a story or an essay? __story__

30

Explain to the pupils what a Coast Guard cutter is and what services it performs.

Become acquainted with the three types of compositions discussed, and be ready to explain the characteristics of each to the class.

Review similes and metaphors, using the examples below.

   (1) Snow sparkles like diamonds. (simile)
   (2) "Israel is an empty vine." (metaphor)
   (3) Kindness is a jewel. (metaphor)
   (4) Her face was as white as a sheet. (simile)

Literary concept in this lesson:

Essays, stories, and poems (Discuss exercise 17 in class.)

Discussion Starters

1. Why did the author include Psalm 107:23, 24 in the essay? (These verses speak of seeing the works and wonders of the Lord at sea. Icebergs are among these works and wonders.)

2. Why do bergs glow with a white light at night? (They reflect every bit of moonlight and starlight that falls on them.)

3. What happens to an iceberg at the end of its journey? (The iceberg breaks into many small pieces that soon melt in the warm ocean water.)

C. Writing for Comprehension

18. What are several ways that icebergs can be dangerous to ships? _____

    Ships can run into the hidden underwater part. Huge splinters can break off and fall

    on ships. Icebergs are often surrounded by fog, which makes it hard to see them.

19. Explain briefly how an iceberg is commonly formed._____

    (Answer should mention the breaking-off process and the place of origin for

    icebergs.)

    _____

The Titanic and an Iceberg

In 1912, a British company built an ocean liner called the *Titanic*. It measured 882 feet long, or about as long as four city blocks. The ship had nine decks on top of each other, which made the ship about as tall as an eleven-story building. Each of its four smokestacks (the fourth was a dummy) stood as high as a large silo and was wide enough to drive a locomotive through. All the engines together produced a total of 50,000 horsepower and consumed about 65 dump truck loads of coal each day.

The British engineers designed the *Titanic* to be unsinkable and called it the "safest ship afloat." One person is even supposed to have said that God Himself could not sink it.

But the ship did sink. On its first trip across the ocean, the *Titanic* came to an area that was thick with icebergs. The icebergs were very hard to see, especially at night, but the captain kept the ship traveling at a high speed. During the night of April 14–15, the ship collided with an iceberg that buckled and cracked the steel plates of the ship's hull. Water gushed in, and in about 2½ hours the ship sank.

Many rich and famous people were on board for this maiden voyage of the *Titanic*. Only 711 of the 2,224 people were rescued. News of this terrible tragedy spread quickly around the world.

Fifth Reader Workbook

 12. The Better Way

Here is your opportunity to write an essay. Putting your own thoughts in writing will help to make you a better reader of what others have written.

Using the main idea suggested by "The Better Way" in your reader, write a three-paragraph essay on a separate paper, telling why it is good to submit to those who are older and wiser than you. Three main ideas are given below to guide your thinking. Write one paragraph for each main idea.

I. Older people have had more experience in life, so they are wiser.

II. Bible characters and other people have left a good example for me.

III. We can follow their example in various ways.

Before you begin your essay, be sure you know the meaning of **submit** and **guidance.** Also study the following list.

Teacher: Do not necessarily insist on rewriting (key 7). Students' essays should use their own words and should be more than a rewording of the main ideas on the outline. Check for content and neatness.

Keys to Good Writing

1. *Think* about what you want to say before you begin writing.

2. *Do not wander* from your main idea.

3. *Be concise.* Do not use more words than necessary.

4. *Be precise.* Use the right words in the right way.

5. *Make sense.* Are your sentences easy to understand? Do they have good grammar?

6. *Work neatly.* Check your spelling and punctuation.

7. *Rewrite* your work until you are satisfied that you have done your best.

Review for Test 2

1. Be sure you know the meanings of the vocabulary words in Lessons 7–12.

2. Be sure you know what these terms mean.

　　figure of speech (Lesson 7)

　　simile (Lesson 7)

　　metaphor (Lesson 7)

　　story (Lesson 11)

　　essay (Lesson 11)

　　poem (Lesson 11)

3. Be sure you know the Keys to Good Writing found in this lesson.

Lesson 12

To the Teacher

This lesson will require much teacher involvement.

After the pupils have read the composition theme, discuss the reasons for the assignment. Point out that there is a relationship between the basic language skills of speaking, listening, writing, and reading.

Some pupils may have difficulty knowing what to write. Class discussion of the questions to the right may help to stimulate their thinking. You may also wish to discuss several reasons for submitting, and list them on the chalkboard. Discuss examples of Bible characters such as Isaac and Jesus, who submitted to their parents.

• Who are some people that are wiser than we?

• How might we receive guidance?

• How can we learn from those who have gone before us, since many of them are no longer living?

Discuss the "Keys to Good Writing." Consider in what way each one is vital, keeping in mind that purpose, discipline, and clarity are essential to successful communication.

Grade the pupils' compositions according to the "Scoring Chart for Compositions" in the section "Checking Students' Work" at the beginning of this teacher's guide.

Literary concept in this lesson:

Composition writing

13. Lito Finds His Way

This story teaches us the value of accepting unfortunate individuals. God does not want His people to make fun of anyone, and especially not those who are crippled or ill. Let us watch for opportunities to show kindness to those who are not blessed in the ways we are. This brings joy not only to them but also to ourselves.

A. Defining for Comprehension

1. The first two paragraphs tell us much about the setting of the story. The word **bamboo** already shows us that the story does not take place in a cold land such as Alaska. Find three other words in the first two paragraphs that show the same thing.
   palm, mango, carabao

2. One of the sentences below contains words with the same meanings as **carabao** and **barrio.** Circle the letter of that sentence. Then rewrite the sentence, replacing those words with **carabao** and **barrio.**

   a. The children from the city liked to listen to the teacher.
   (b.) The boy rode his buffalo into their city district.
   c. The caravan arrived at the oasis.
   The boy rode his carabao into their barrio.

3. Circle the letter of the word below that best describes Lito's feeling about his crippled leg and ragged clothes at the beginning of the story.
   a. concern   b. pride   (c.) shame   d. sorrow

4. The other children were sitting in a semicircle. What is a semicircle? a half circle

B. Reading for Comprehension

5. a. This story takes place in what country? Philippines

   b. Which other story that you studied in this reader takes place in that country?
      "To Market"

6. Circle the letter of the sentence that gives the main reason why Lito was afraid to join the Bible school children.

   a. Lito was afraid the children would know his father.
   b. Lito was afraid that the children would stare at him.
   (c.) Lito was afraid that the children would tease him.

7. Part of Proverbs 17:5 says that if we mock the poor, we are finding fault with God Himself. Write the part of the verse which says that.
   "Whoso mocketh the poor reproacheth his Maker."

33

Lesson 13

To the Teacher

Before having the pupils read this story orally, review the principles of good reading: read clearly and distinctly, use proper voice inflection, observe punctuation marks, practice good elocution, and read loudly enough so that everyone can hear. Encourage each student to put forth his best effort in reading this story.

A carabao (kăr ə bou′) is a small water buffalo used as a draft animal in the Philippines. A barrio (bä′ rē ō)—from the Spanish word for "neighborhood"—is one of the districts into which the cities are divided. Apparently Miss Naomi was teaching at a church in a different barrio than the one where Lito lived.

Discuss what it would be like to see the world through Lito's eyes as he saw it in the first half of the story. Ask the students if they have ever been teased or made fun of. How did it make them feel? Ask them what it feels like to be left out of play and other activities with children of their own age.

After reading the story, discuss the difference in these children's attitudes toward Lito as compared with the attitudes of those who ridiculed him.

Point out that people can usually tell very soon whether we accept or reject them. It is a serious thing when rejection by religious people turns someone away from God. Help the pupils to sense their responsibility to include everyone in their play, in group conversations, or in whatever they do as a group.

Fifth Reader Workbook

8. The *main character* of a story is the main person that the story is about. This person is the center of the things that happen in the story.
   a. Who is the main character in this story? _____ Lito _____
   b. Who is the second most important character? _____ Miss Naomi _____

9. Notice Lito's progress in coming to the Bible school class.
   a. Where had he stood the day before to watch the class? __ across the road __
   b. Where was he standing at the beginning of the story? __ at the fence __
   c. Where was he standing when he joined the class? __ in the semicircle __
      (or under the mango tree)

10. When Lito saw the picture of the boy on crutches, he suddenly moved over to the churchyard gate. Circle the letter of the sentence below that best tells why he did this.
   (a.) Lito was crippled like the boy in the picture.
   b. Lito liked brightly colored pictures.
   c. Lito liked Miss Naomi's kind voice.

11. Notice that Miss Naomi said nothing about Lito's tattered clothing or crippled leg, but she spoke favorably of something he could do well. What was that?
   __ his singing __

C. Writing for Comprehension

12. Write a paragraph describing Lito's father and telling why the family may have been poor because of him. __ (Paragraph should mention the father's laziness and his wasting of __ time and money on cockfights.) __
   _____
   _____
   _____

13. By accepting him into their group, how did Lito's new friends help him? Whom else did they help? Explain. __ (Sample points to be mentioned.) __
   __ Lito's new friends helped him by making him feel welcome at Bible school, where __
   __ he learned about God. His family was also helped because they started going to __
   __ church. His father probably quit wasting his money and started supporting the __
   __ family better. An observant student may also recognize that these things brought __
   __ joy to Lito's new friends. __

34

Literary concept in this lesson:

Main character (Discuss exercise 8 in class.)

Discussion Starters

1. What were some things Lito was often teased about? (his ragged clothes, his mended crutches, his useless leg, his skinny dog, his shiftless father, his lack of schooling)
2. The story says that Lito's house was the shakiest one in the barrio. How could a house be shaky? (A shaky house would not be solid and sturdy. Its floors and walls could be shaken with little effort.)
3. Was Lito a bad boy? How do you know? (No. He came to the Bible school even though he used crutches and was afraid the other children would laugh at him.)
4. How did the song help Lito? (It helped him to overcome his shyness and come close enough to join in the singing.)
5. How did the children show that they cared about Lito? (They smiled at Lito and welcomed him to their Bible school. They did not make fun of him.)
6. How did the teacher know Lito's name? (She asked one of the girls in the class.)
7. Why had Lito never gone to school? (because of his crutches, his shabby clothes, and the cost of schoolbooks)

14. My Childhood in Scotland

The author of this story was reflecting on her life as a young girl in Scotland. Memories of the pleasant experiences she had in her carefree childhood days held a special place in her mind. The challenge for you is to be cheerful and obedient today so that you can also learn good habits and have many pleasant memories later in life.

A. Defining for Comprehension

Write the letter of the matching definition before each word.

c	1. melancholy	a.	Took apart.
f	2. adjoining	b.	Safety; protection; assurance.
g	3. cubicles	c.	Sad; depressed in spirit.
l	4. utensils	d.	Appealing; tempting.
a	5. dismantled	e.	Glow; brightness.
e	6. luster	f.	Directly connected; in contact with.
h	7. fared	g.	Small partitioned spaces, as for sleeping or study.
k	8. vendors	h.	Got along; were supplied.
d	9. tantalizing	i.	Supported; strengthened.
j	10. array	j.	Arrangement; assortment.
i	11. sustained	k.	People who sell items; peddlers.
b	12. security	l.	Kitchen tools, such as knives and spoons.

13. The author says that her house had a slate roof and that she did her school work on a slate. A piece of slate is a thin layer of (plastic, cardboard, <u>rock,</u> wood).

14. Rewrite the sentence below, replacing the underlined words with their meanings as given in the footnotes of the story. (Footnotes appear in small print at the bottom of a page.)

There was a <u>tinny</u> on the <u>grate</u> in the <u>bothy</u> at the end of the <u>byre</u> in the <u>glen</u>.

There was a mug on the fireplace in the farmhand's apartment at the end of the cow stable in the valley.

_____

35

Lesson 14

To the Teacher

Introduce the lesson by showing the students on a map where Scotland is located.

As the pupils read the story orally, on the chalkboard draw the floor plan of the Young's home in Scotland. Divide the floor area into two parts. In the front area, draw the two cubicles that were built into the wall. Show the boys' bed and the large wardrobe in the back room. Add the grate in the central part of the front room, and show the bucket behind the door.

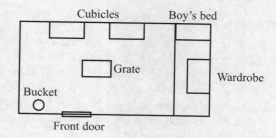

Fifth Reader Workbook

B. Reading for Comprehension

15. Were you concentrating on details as you read this story? Without looking back, write whether each sentence below is true (**T**) or false (**F**). Then look back and correct any wrong answers.

   __T__   a. Most of the workmen in Greengairs were coal miners.

   __F__   b. A stone dyke is a ditch to carry water.

   __F__   c. The author's childhood home had three rooms.

   __T__   d. Four families shared the water faucet in the yard.

   __F__   e. The family in the story had their own milk cow.

   __T__   f. A burn is a brook.

   __T__   g. The family attended church on Sundays.

16. According to the first paragraph of the story, "it is the joyful memories which follow us through the years, while the melancholy scenes fade into the background." Circle the letter of the sentence below that says most nearly the same thing.

   a. We tend to remember our unpleasant experiences and forget the pleasant ones.

   (b.) We tend to carry pleasant memories with us and leave the unpleasant ones behind.

   c. Our memories grow worse as we grow older, and we tend to forget the things that happened in the past.

17. Circle the letter of the sentence that gives the writer's purpose for this story.

   (a.) The author wanted to describe her life in Scotland as a child.

   b. The author wanted to show how she learned to become thrifty with water.

   c. The author wanted to tell what games she played as a child.

36

The Young's lifestyle was very simple compared to most of ours. Discuss with the students the advantages of a simple lifestyle. Point out that life without modern conveniences was much more difficult, but it had rich rewards as the family worked together to get large tasks done.

As an alternate activity, you may want to have your students write a composition about a part of their lives such as usual Sunday activities or a typical school day.

Literary concept in this lesson:

Fiction and nonfiction (Discuss exercise 18 in class.)

Discussion Starters

1. Why does the story say the front room was a true living room? (The family members did most of their living in this room—cooking, eating, working, playing, and sleeping.)

2. Why did they save the bedding and table linens for the laundry man to wash? (Apparently this was the most convenient way to get these items washed.)

3. Do you think the author liked soup? Why or why not? (No. In explaining why rainy and winter washdays were dreaded, the author says they almost always had soup on those days.)

6. Did they go shopping in town? (There was little need for this because of the "never-ending stream of vendors"— the milkman, the butcher, the baker, the coal man, the paraffin man, and an occasional fish vendor.)

18. If an author writes about imaginary characters and events, his composition is called *fiction.* A story is fiction if it is fabricated (made up). But if an author writes about things that actually happened, the composition is **nonfiction.** Whether a composition is fiction or nonfiction, it should teach a worthwhile lesson or discuss a worthwhile subject.

Write whether each sentence describes fiction (**F**) or nonfiction (**N**).

N   a. The story of a person's life.

N   b. A letter to a friend.

F   c. A story written from your imagination.

N   d. An account of an accident.

F   e. A story with make-believe characters.

C. Writing for Comprehension

19. a. What is meant by the statement that "grief befell" anyone who tore or rumpled the curtains?
    It means that person was punished.

b. Why do you think her mother cared so much about those curtains? (Sample answers.)
    The family had very few pretty things. Also, the curtains were needed for privacy and would have been hard to replace.

20. How do you think the teacher could tell when the mothers helped the girls with their scarves?
    The part done by a mother was probably knitted more tightly and neatly.

21. Near the end of the story, the author tells us that not everything in her childhood was pleasant. Find and write the part of a sentence that says this.
    Of course, when I was young, the heather did not bloom every day in Scotland.

22. What was one good habit the author learned in her childhood that she remembered the rest of her life?
    to be thrifty with water

37

4. Name some of their toys and the games they played. (The girls played house with homemade stocking dolls, and they rolled hoops obtained from barrels. They also skipped rope and played with marbles and jacks. The boys used barrel hoops to make kites, and they played "rounders." All the children played with tops called peeries, and they played kick-the-can, run-sheep-run, hide-the-thimble, and I-spy.)
5. What did the family do on Sundays? What can we learn from this? (They played no games on Sundays, and they attended church and Sunday school. They visited their grandparents, friends, and neighbors, and often several families sang hymns together. This shows their respect for the Lord's Day.)

Fifth Reader Workbook

15. The Security of the Righteous

Psalm 91 is a beautiful example of Bible poetry. In the reader it is arranged in stanzas to help you see that it is a poem. This psalm promises protection and deliverance to those who trust in God. Its message has brought comfort to many people.

A. Defining for Comprehension

Study the meanings of these words from Psalm 91. Then use them to fill in the blanks in the paragraph below. You will not use all the words.

> fowler—a person who traps birds
> noisome—destructive; dangerous
> pestilence—plague
> buckler—a small shield
> wasteth—destroys; ruins
> habitation—dwelling place; residence
> befall—happen to
> adder—a poisonous snake; viper
> fortress—a safe place for soldiers

One day a (1)___**fowler**___ went out to trap birds, carrying a small shield or (2)___**buckler**___ with him. He knew that the forest could be (3)___**noisome**___ and that something harmful could (4)___**befall**___ him. The first thing he met was an (5)___**adder**___, which tried to bite him. He killed it quickly and said to himself, "A dangerous creature like that is a (6)___**pestilence**___ that (7)___**wasteth**___ him who hath been bitten by it." He caught some birds and then returned to his (8)___**habitation**___.
(or fortress)

B. Reading for Comprehension

9. Bible poetry does not have the rhyme and rhythm that we find in most poems. But it is still poetry because it is written in a poetic style. Many of the lines are about the same length. Also, the thought of one line is often similar to the thought of the line before or after it. So instead of rhyming words, the lines have "rhyming thoughts." A poem of this kind can be recognized as poetry even if it is translated to another language. Lines with "rhyming thoughts" and similar structure are called ***parallel lines.***

38

Lesson 15

To the Teacher

In this lesson, Psalm 91 is arranged according to the form generally used for poetry. (The Hebrew arrangement is much the same.) This pattern should help the students to recognize the psalm more readily as being a poem.

Notice the many parallel lines in this psalm: stanza 3, lines 3 and 4; stanza 4, lines 2, 3, and 4; stanza 5, lines 1 and 2; stanza 6, lines 1 and 2; and so forth. Also observe the many related words in adjacent lines: stanza 1, *dwelleth* and *abide*; stanza 3, *feathers* and *wings*; stanza 4, *pestilence* and *destruction*; and many more. These related words are major elements that contribute to the parallelism in the psalm.

Tell the pupils that this poem is more worthwhile than many other compositions because it is the Word of God. (See Discussion Starters, number 1.) There is a serene beauty in its lines that is well worth the effort it takes to discover. Its message of trust and security has brought comfort and consolation to many a weary soul.

Do much of this lesson as a class if possible, especially parts A and C.

Literary concepts in this lesson:

Parallel lines (See exercise 9.)
Imagery (See exercise 10.)
Poetry versus prose (See exercise 11.)

Copy the parallel lines described below, which you find in the poem. A clue is given for each set.

a. stanza 4 (three lines): Harmful things that the righteous need not fear.

<u>Nor for the arrow that flieth by day;</u>

<u>Nor for the pestilence that walketh in darkness;</u>

<u>Nor for the destruction that wasteth at noonday.</u>

b. stanza 5 (two lines): Many people nearby will be harmed (but not the righteous).

<u>A thousand shall fall at thy side,</u>

<u>And ten thousand at thy right hand.</u>

c. last stanza (two lines): God will be near the righteous in difficult times.

<u>I will be with him in trouble;</u>

<u>I will deliver him, and honour him.</u>

10. The third stanza has *imagery,* or a word picture, which describes God as caring for His people like a hen caring for her chicks. Copy the two lines that suggest this.

<u>He shall cover thee with his feathers,</u>

<u>And under his wings shalt thou trust.</u>

11. The two main kinds of composition are poetry and prose. *Poetry* is usually arranged in lines and stanzas with rhyming words or thoughts. *Prose* is any kind of writing that is not poetry, such as stories and essays.

Read the following sentences about poetry and prose, and write whether each one is true (**T**) or false (**F**).

<u>T</u>   a. Many of the hymns we sing are poetry set to music.

<u>F</u>   b. A short story would most likely be written as a poem.

<u>T</u>   c. An article about Christian homes would be prose.

<u>F</u>   d. Prose is written in stanzas.

<u>F</u>   e. Prose usually contains rhyming words.

<u>T</u>   f. The Bible contains some poetry.

Discussion Starters

1. Why is this the best poem you have had so far in this reader? (It is from the Word of God.)

2. What are some things God protects us from? (The psalm mentions the following: the snare of the fowler, the noisome [destructive] pestilence, the terror by night, the arrow by day, the pestilence of darkness, the destruction of noonday, the plague, the lion, the adder, the young lion, and the dragon [a fierce creature of uncertain identity]. Discuss some possible applications in our lives. (Some call this the Traveler's Psalm.)

3. What do the angels do for the righteous? (The angels keep [preserve] the righteous and bear them up, "lest [they] dash [their] foot against a stone.")

4. Which lines say that we do not need to fear danger at night? ("Thou shalt not be afraid for the terror by night; . . . nor for the pestilence that walketh in darkness.")

Fifth Reader Workbook

12. How should this psalm make the reader feel? Circle the letter of the best answer.

    a. sober and thoughtful

    (b.) encouraged and grateful

    c. thrilled and delighted

    d. guilty and fearful

C. Writing for Comprehension

13. Write the main idea of this psalm in one sentence of your own. Consider the introductory paragraph if you need help.

    God protects and delivers those who trust Him.

14. In the first stanza, "most High" and "Almighty" are used as names for God. What do these names tell us about God?

    "Most High" tells us that God is above all else.

    "Almighty" tells us that God is greater and stronger than all else.

D. Review

Fill in the blanks.

15. A semicircle is _____half_____ of a circle.

16. The word **tantalizing** means "___appealing___ or ___tempting___."

17. A story is called ___nonfiction___ if it tells about something that really happened.

18. A story is called ___fiction___ if it tells about imaginary characters and events.

16. Danger in the Wind

This story shows God's instant response to prayer in time of emergency. It is important that we always give Him the glory for His protection, as Stewart did in this story.

A. Defining for Comprehension

1. This story has many ***mood words*** that help to produce a calm feeling at the beginning of the story and an exciting mood or feeling later. Below is a list of mood words from the story. Write whether each word suggests a feeling of calmness (**C**) or excitement (**E**).

   _E_ a. fearful   _E_ i. anxiety

   _C_ b. tranquil   _E_ j. desperately

   _C_ c. drifted   _E_ k. raced

   _E_ d. startled   _E_ l. attacked

   _C_ e. breeze   _C_ m. weary

   _C_ f. smoldering   _E_ n. roared

   _E_ g. lunging   _C_ o. soberly

   _E_ h. alarm

Circle the letter of the best definition for each of these words from the story.

2. volunteers   a. those who help quickly   (b.) those who offer to help
3. supervise   (a.) give directions to   b. help
4. summoned   a. informed   (b.) called
5. extinguished   (a.) put out   b. slowed down
6. anxious   a. eager   (b.) worried

B. Reading for Comprehension

7. A good story or essay captures the reader's attention from the very beginning. So it is important that the ***opening paragraph*** is interesting. One way that an opening paragraph arouses interest is by suggesting that something exciting or unusual is coming later in the composition.

   Copy the sentence from the opening paragraph of "Danger in the Wind" that makes the reader think something exciting will soon happen.

   It was such a peaceful, tranquil day that no one in the little Oregon school guessed the fearful excitement that was to come.

Lesson 16

To the Teacher

After reading the first several paragraphs with the class, discuss various indications of a peaceful day. What sights, sounds, and smells did Stewart observe? (Examples: a hummingbird hovering outside the window, the grass turning green, the neighbor plowing)

Read on to where Brother Jonathan asked for volunteers to clean the schoolyard. Ask the pupils why they think everyone was so willing to cooperate. (See Discussion Starters, number 4.)

Point out the buildup of excitement as the story progresses. Ask the pupils to find some words that tell how the characters felt. (Examples: anxiously, desperately, excitedly)

After the class has read the story, discuss lessons we can learn from it, such as dependence on God, being content with things as they are, and giving God the glory for answered prayer.

Discuss exercise 14 in class. Use this opportunity to teach rules of fire safety.

Literary concept in this lesson:

Mood words (Discuss exercise 1 in class.)
Opening paragraph (Discuss exercise 7 in class.)

Fifth Reader Workbook

8. Who said, "See what glorious things God has made"? Think carefully, and then circle the letter of the correct answer.

    a. Brother Jonathan

    b. Stewart

    c. A hummingbird

    d. Charles

    (e.) No one

    Teacher: A hummingbird only seemed to say this.

9. What did Brother Jonathan tell the boys to do before he lit the fire, which shows that he was trying to be very careful? _____

    He told them to get wet sacks to keep the fire under control.

10. The following sentences are based on sentences in the story. Without looking back, number them in the correct order. Then look back and correct any wrong answers.

    _5_   a. Brother Jonathan knelt and applied a match to the dry grass.

    _2_   b. Startled, Stewart hastily turned to his work again.

    _9_   c. "We're gaining!" shouted Charles.

    _8_   d. "O dear God, please show us what to do."

    _4_   e. The two boys exchanged questioning glances.

    _10_ f. "No," Stewart said, "the credit goes to God."

    _1_   g. Fresh smells of spring drifted in the open windows.

    _7_   h. They were getting nowhere. The wind was rising.

    _3_   i. Outside in the yard, the students were grouped and given tasks.

    _6_   j. Then it happened! The breeze came very suddenly.

11. What one thing, more than anything else, caused the fire to spread out of control?

    the wind

12. What thought came to Stewart's mind after he prayed? _____

    He thought of fighting the fire at the lane that ran through the woods.

13. How do you know that Stewart was a humble boy?   He said, "The credit goes to God."
    Also, he did not challenge the teacher.

42

Discussion Starters

1. Where does the story take place? (in Oregon)
2. What jobs did the teacher give the little children? the older girls? Stewart and Charles? (*little children:* picking up litter; *older girls:* supervising the little children and emptying wastebaskets; *Stewart and Charles:* helping to burn dead grass; keeping the fire under control)
3. Were there many students in this school? How do you know? (No. The first sentence says it was a little school. The group was so small that it took two hours to extinguish the last flames.)
4. Why were the children so excited about outdoor cleanup? (It was a very warm day to be studying in the classroom.)
5. Does God always answer prayer immediately as He did for Stewart? (No, but in an emergency like this He often does.)
6. Why is "Danger in the Wind" a good title? (It makes the reader wonder what the story is about. It fits well because the wind caused the danger.)

C. Writing for Comprehension

14. Write a paragraph telling why it is important to be very careful with fire. For a few ideas, consider the many things fire can destroy, including life.

   (Paragraph should mention the possibility of fire destroying buildings, trees, animals, and even people's lives. It would be good to discuss this subject before assigning the exercise.)

   _____

   _____

D. Review

Underline the correct answers.

15. The main character in "Danger in the Wind" is (<u>Stewart,</u> Charles).

16. A story about imaginary characters and events is called (<u>fiction</u>, nonfiction).

17. "Danger in the Wind" is the kind of composition called (poetry, <u>prose</u>).

Fifth Reader Workbook

 # 17. Outdoor Good Manners

This essay shows how selfish it is to litter or destroy public parks and campsites. God made nature to be enjoyed by all men. It is wrong for us to ruin what belongs to everyone by being careless with it. Since nature is a gift from God, we are responsible to Him for how we use it.

A. Defining for Comprehension

Write the letter of the matching definition before each word.

_e_	1. strewn	a. Decided firmly; determined.
_a_	2. resolved	b. Completely; unquestionably.
_j_	3. frequent	c. Hold dear; prize.
_i_	4. situated	d. Careless; thoughtless.
_f_	5. individuals	e. Covered with scattered things.
_b_	6. absolutely	f. Persons.
_d_	7. negligent	g. Demonstration; show.
_g_	8. display	h. Recognize the value of.
_c_	9. cherish	i. Placed; located.
_h_	10. appreciate	j. Visit often.

Fill in the blanks in this sentence with words from the list above.

11. Alvin ___resolved___ that he would not be ___negligent___ with his responsibility to keep the park clean.

B. Reading for Comprehension

12. According to 1 Timothy 6:17, who gives us all things to enjoy? ___God___

13. The third paragraph may sound rather amusing and not true to life. But when people display poor manners outdoors, it is very much the way the author describes it. Circle the letter of the phrase below that best describes the attitudes of people with outdoor bad manners.

    a. considerate and careless

    b. unselfish and impolite

    (c.) thoughtless and inconsiderate

14. What is meant by the phrase "the world on wheels"? _____

    ___people traveling in cars___

44

Lesson 17

To the Teacher

Contrast the anticipation of going on a picnic with the disappointment of finding the campgrounds littered with debris from others' picnics. The Golden Rule can be applied here very appropriately. Also bring in our responsibility as stewards of God's earth.

See how many reasons the pupils can find in the lesson for practicing good manners outdoors. Pupils' reasons should include such things as neatness, preventing forest fires, and not attracting ants and bears.

You may wish to have the students make posters illustrating good outdoor manners, or have them work together on a bulletin board on this theme.

Discussion Starters

1. Name some things people would probably not do at home or at a neighbor's house, which they often do in a park. (They would not throw dishes on the floor or the ground; dump banana skins, eggshells, and tin cans on the floor or the ground; or leave a fire burning when it could cause great destruction.)

2. What does this composition say that reminds you of the story "Danger in the Wind"? (It says that a sudden breeze may fan live coals into a blaze that starts a forest fire.)

3. If you ever pick a wildflower, how should you do it? (Pick it carefully without pulling up the roots.)

15. What large animals can become a nuisance if garbage is left at a park? bears

16. What unhealthy habit of many people can cause forest fires? smoking

17. Why is it thoughtless to pick beautiful flowers at public parks?

    They will no longer be there for others to enjoy.

18. Read the following sentence: A little extra time and care spent with campfires can prevent many trees from being destroyed and many animals or even people from being burned.

    Now copy the sentence from the essay that means about the same but uses fewer words.

    An ounce of prevention in putting out a campfire may save a great deal of loss and

    suffering. (Note: Older editions of the reader have *protection* instead of *prevention*.)

19. What are some results of outdoor bad manners? List at least four of them from the essay.

    (Sample answers.) Garbage strewn about looks untidy,

    draws flies, spreads disease, and attracts bears.

    It takes money and time to clean up garbage.

    Destructive forest fires may result.

C. Writing for Comprehension

20. Explain how a bed of ashes can be innocent-looking yet dangerous.

    A bed of ashes may look dead while still smoldering underneath.

    The wind can fan live coals into a blaze.

21. What can be done to make sure a campfire is completely extinguished?

    Water can be poured on the fire, or soil can be thrown over it.

D. Review

22. The _____main_____ _____idea_____ of this essay is that it is selfish to harm public parks and campsites.

23. Words that give feelings to a story are called _____mood_____ words.

24. The _____opening_____ _____paragraph_____ of a composition should be interesting so the reader will want to read the rest of it.

45

4. What is meant by the sentence that says, "Good manners should not be put on and off"? (We should practice good manners at all times and places.)

5. In your own words, give a list of outdoor manners. (The three main rules in this essay are as follows: [1] Clean up all garbage and rubbish. [2] Be sure any fire is completely put out. [3] Do not pick plants and flowers. Ask pupils to suggest other rules.)

Fifth Reader Workbook

 ## 18. The Crop of Acorns

This poem teaches an important lesson. Our hearts are like a field ready to be sown with the seeds of good or bad habits. Satan wants to place little bad "seeds" into our "soil." Bad habits, like acorns, may seem small and harmless, but as we let them grow, they become like huge oak trees. We must root out bad habits early in our lives, and develop good habits in their place.

A. Defining for Comprehension

This poem is a bit hard to understand because of the way some words are used. Write a line from the poem that matches the thought of each phrase or sentence below.

1. And gently told what he wanted

   And urged his suit in accents meek

2. The landlord was not sure that it was a good idea.

   The owner some misgivings felt.

3. And smooth urging persuade

   And honeyed argument prevail

4. Then grew large, spreading boughs

   Then broad and wide their branches threw

5. Do not make any deals; turn down the offer.

   No bargains make—reject the suit.

6. Decide firmly that you will not be caught in the harmful trap.

   With firmness break the evil snare.

7. Write a definition for each word below. Use your dictionary.

   a. vice   bad behavior; bad habit

   b. tenant   person who pays rent to use property

   c. lease   agreement by which an owner rents out property

B. Reading for Comprehension

8. What was the "one crop" that the tenant wanted to plant?   oak trees (acorns)

9. a. The owner was expecting to lease the field for (<u>one year</u>, more than one year).

   b. The tenant was expecting to rent the field for (one year, <u>more than one year</u>).

Circle the letter of the best choice.

10. In the second stanza, **stranger** refers to

    a. God.   b. Satan.   c. a person.

46

Lesson 18

To the Teacher

Discuss the similarities between habits and acorns. Both seem small and harmless, yet if they are allowed to develop, they will eventually grow beyond our control. Point out that the owner is like each of us as individuals, and that the tenant (renter) is like Satan.

This is a good lesson to practice paraphrasing. Encourage the students to use the dictionary freely in completing the exercises. You should discuss exercise 15 in class, but be careful that students formulate answers in their own words.

If possible, tell the story of this poem in an interesting way before the students read the poem. "The Crop of Acorns"

in the reader *Seeking True Values* (from Pathway Publishers) is a narrative version of the poem.

Discussion Starters

1. What are some careless habits that we should break? (Answers will vary.)
2. What are some good habits to plant? (Answers will vary.)
3. What is the field or garden that the poem talks about? (our hearts or souls)
4. Why is "one crop" in the second stanza in quotation marks? (It emphasizes the "one crop alone" that the tenant sought. It also indicates the irony of the situation—"one crop" indeed, but what a crop!)
5. Did the landlord die before the crop was grown? How do

11. In the third stanza, **landlord** refers to
    a. God.   b. Satan.   c. a person.

12. In the last stanza, **sun-excluding grove** refers to
    a. a forest.
    b. a cloud covering the sun.
    c. a multitude of enslaving habits.

13. The message of this poem is mainly for
    a. young people.   b. middle-aged people.   c. old people.

14. Instead of using thistle seeds to illustrate bad habits, the writer of this poem used the seeds of oak trees (acorns). He did this because
    a. acorns are larger than thistle seeds.
    b. acorns can grow into big trees that last a long time.
    c. acorns do not spread as rapidly as thistle seeds.

C. Writing for Comprehension

15. Rewrite the first stanza in prose, using your own words. (Sample paragraph.)

    One day many years ago, a stranger came to a farmer to rent a piece of land. He meekly insisted that he would raise only one crop and then return the field to the farmer.

D. Review for Test 3

16. Be sure you know the meanings of the vocabulary words in Lessons 13–18.

17. Be sure you know what these terms mean.

    main character (Lesson 13)
    fiction and nonfiction (Lesson 14)
    parallel lines (Lesson 15)
    imagery (Lesson 15)
    poetry and prose (Lesson 15)
    mood words (Lesson 16)
    opening paragraph (Lesson 16)

you know? (Yes. The third stanza says that long before the oaks reached their prime, the cheated landlord lay in his grave.)

Fifth Reader Workbook

 ## 19. A Night on the Mississippi

As you grow older, you will have the experience of doing various things for the first time, such as making a meal by yourself or driving the tractor to plow a field. Such experiences can be adventures for you, just as the first night on the Mississippi River was for the boy in this story. As you read, notice the many descriptive words and phrases that help us to "see" things with the author and share in his experience.

A. Defining for Comprehension

Use the following words from the story to fill in the blanks below. Seeing how the words are used in the story should help you to use them correctly. You will use all the words except one.

snag	astonished	familiar	trackless
unwieldy	drowsy	bluffs	towhead
skiff	infinite	poised	stroke

1. God has created an ___infinite___ number of stars.

2. The fisherman's ___skiff___ was stuck on a ___towhead___ or ___snag___ in the middle of the river.

3. The bird flew through the ___trackless___ sky to its winter home.

4. The big, ___unwieldy___ truck was hard to keep on the road.

5. Steep ___bluffs___ rose at the edge of the lake.

6. The wary chipmunk was ___poised___ to run at the first sign of danger.

7. George could easily find his way because he was in ___familiar___ territory.

8. Amy was ___astonished___ when she saw how many people had come.

9. Paul split the log with one ___stroke___ of his axe.

10. Write a sentence of your own, using the one remaining word in the same way it is used in the story. ___(Pupil's sentence should use *drowsy* to mean "sleepy.")___

48

Lesson 19

To the Teacher

This is an adventure story, but it is not the usual kind. It is not filled with suspense or brave deeds, neither does it have an exciting plot or a breathtaking climax. Rather, it is a simple but enjoyable story of a young boy's first night out on the Mississippi River.

Insist that the students read with proper expression, paying attention to the punctuation.

As the story progresses, draw the students' attention to the vivid, picturesque words. For example, ask how the sights looked along the river, and how the breaking of day is described. This will help them to visualize the story as mentioned in exercise 18.

Compare the river trip with Columbus's voyage. How were they alike? How were they different? Point out the Mississippi River on a map.

In connection with the last part of the story, ask the students if they have had the experience of seeing something happen and then hearing the sound a moment later. Explain why this happens. (See Discussion Starters, number 5.)

Discuss exercise 18. Tell the students whether to write a paragraph or draw a sketch.

Literary concepts in this lesson:

Narrator versus author (See exercise 12.)
Visualizing (See exercise 18.)

B. Reading for Comprehension

11. Circle the letter of the year when this story most likely took place. Then write why each of the other two years is not a good choice.

    a. 1610   (b.) 1890   c. 1975   (Sample reasons.)

    In 1610 no steamboats existed, nor any river traffic as described in the story.

    In 1975 people did not use rafts and steamboats as described in the story.

12. The person who tells a story is called the **narrator.** In this story, the narrator is also the main character. This makes the story especially interesting because it is a first-hand account.

    a. How old was the narrator at the time of this story? __thirteen__

    b. Is his name given in the story? __no__

13. How was the main character like Christopher Columbus? Circle the letter of the best answer.

    a. They both liked sailing.

    (b.) They both went on a new adventure.

    c. They both performed outstanding deeds.

    d. They both steered their vessels.

14. a. What mood does this story have? Circle the letter of the best description below.

    a. sad   (b.) peaceful   c. exciting

    b. Now find the paragraph that begins with these words: "As the shadows grew longer." Copy at least five words from that paragraph which help to produce the mood of the story.

    __(Any five.) drowsy, soft, fanned, gently, lap, soothing, asleep, quiet__

15. The Mississippi River follows a winding course. Copy phrases from the paragraphs indicated below that confirm this fact.

    a. paragraph 6 __a curve in the river soon hid him from sight__

    b. paragraph 11 __a bend of the stream would hide their lights__

16. a. Read the last phrase of Romans 12:13. What is hospitality? _____

    __friendliness toward strangers or kind care for guests__

    b. How did the boys show hospitality?_____

    __They shared their supper with the trapper and gave him a place to sleep.__

Discussion Starters

1. Why were the story characters going down the Mississippi? (to take some crops to market)
2. At one spot on the raft they piled dirt five or six inches deep. Why? (as a place to build a fire)
3. Were they traveling upstream or downstream? How do you know? (They were traveling downstream. The first sentence says "down the Mississippi River." They drifted along on a raft. One sentence says "as if they too were floating downstream.")
4. What did the author do when it was his turn to steer? Why? (He kept the raft on a winding course for half an hour. He did that "for the mere fun of it.")
5. Why did he see the man's axe hit the wood before he heard the sound? (Light travels much faster than sound. Because the man was some distance away, the author saw the action a moment before he heard the sound.)

Fifth Reader Workbook

C. Writing for Comprehension

17. The boys faced some dangers while rafting down the Mississippi. Describe two of the dangers that the story mentions, and tell what precautions the boys took against them.

   a.   Their steering oar might break, so James made some extra oars.

   _____

   _____

   b.   Their raft might be run down by a steamboat, so they hung a lantern on a forked

      stick. _____

   _____

   _____

   _____

   _____

   _____

18. A good author uses many descriptive words that help you see in your mind the events and scenes in a story. This seeing in your mind is called *visualizing.* In this story you can visualize the raft by how it is described. Write a paragraph about the raft, or draw a sketch of it, as your teacher tells you.

   (Sample sketch is shown. Paragraph should mention the cabin and fireplace on the raft, and should be in the pupils' own words.)

50

20. Looking at the Other Side

Many children in the world today are hurting because of unfaithful adults in their lives. Nevertheless, there are also godly people who care much about children. It is important that children learn to trust those who truly care about them, even when correction is necessary.

A. Defining for Comprehension

Match the following words from the story with their definitions. If you need help with a word, see how it is used in the story or find it in a dictionary.

Part I

_i_	1. stealthily	a.	Carefully looking over.
_l_	2. reluctantly	b.	Perplexity; confusion.
_g_	3. asserted	c.	Roads; highways.
_a_	4. scanning	d.	Stealing.
_f_	5. urchin	e.	Determined; steadfast.
_c_	6. thoroughfares	f.	Mischievous child.
_d_	7. filching	g.	Stated firmly; declared.
_b_	8. bewilderment	h.	Plan for doing things at regular times.
_e_	9. resolute	i.	Secretly; sneakily.
_k_	10. wary	j.	Made more bold.
_h_	11. schedule	k.	Cautious; on guard.
_m_	12. stifling	l.	Unwillingly; hesitantly.
_j_	13. emboldened	m.	Choking; oppressive.

Part II

_o_	14. scrounge	n.	Compelled; driven.
_n_	15. constrained	o.	Obtain by searching or begging.
_r_	16. bedraggled	p.	For a brief time.
_q_	17. objections	q.	Arguments against something.
_p_	18. momentarily	r.	Wet and untidy.

Lesson 20

To the Teacher

This story lends itself especially well to oral reading. Be sure the students read in a way that expresses the feelings of the characters—anxious, sad, angry.

Point out El Salvador on a map. Tell the pupils that it is a country in Central America and that San Salvador is its capital.

Be sure the students understand why Armando (är män′ dō) mistrusted adults. In his early years he had not had a proper relationship with any adult.

Talk about the advantages and disadvantages of having been taken into the Muñozes' home. Point out that privileges often bring responsibilities with them.

Discuss the kindness and patience shown by both Brother Montealegre (môn tä ä lĕg′ rā) and the Muñozes, and the redemptive effect this had on Armando.

Emphasize that in almost every misunderstanding, there are two sides to the issue. Perhaps you can tell the class about a misunderstanding in your own experience.

Have the students contrast Armando's attitudes at the beginning of the story with those he displayed at the end. What brought about the great change?

Remember to help students with at least some of the vocabulary words.

Fifth Reader Workbook

B. Reading for Comprehension

19. Why did Brother Montealegre think Armando might have stolen the money? Give two reasons.

   Armando had previously been guilty of stealing.

   Rodrigo had lost about the same amount that Armando had.

20. How had Armando actually gotten the money?   by chopping weeds

21. For what main reason had Armando become suspicious of anyone much older than himself? Circle the letter of the best answer.

   a. Armando did not know anything about his parents.

   b. His life with the Muñozes seemed too restrictive.

   (c.) A number of adults had deceived him in the past.

   d. Many of the people he knew were not Christians.

22. Why had Brother Montealegre tied Armando's horse by the schoolhouse door?

   a. Brother Montealegre was trying to get even with Armando.

   (b.) Brother Montealegre wanted to talk with Armando.

   c. Brother Montealegre feared that Armando in his anger would mistreat the horse.

   d. For all the reasons given above.

23. Why did Armando return to the Muñozes after running away from school?

   a. The city was too far away.

   b. The Muñozes had showed him loving care.

   c. He was cold and hungry.

   (d.) For all these reasons.

24. Armando was expecting to be scolded and punished when he got home, but the Muñozes showed only kindness to him. Read Proverbs 15:1. Then decide which of the following feelings Armando would most likely have had if the Muñozes had scolded him harshly.

   (a.) Anger; ready to argue.

   b. Contrition; ready to beg forgiveness.

   c. Regret; sorry for what he had done.

25. At the beginning of the story, Armando thought that all grownups were against him. How much did this wrong idea have to do with his problems in the story?

   a. nothing at all

   b. a little

   (c.) very much

52

Discussion Starters

1. What is the first indication in the story that Armando had truly earned the money? (A sentence in paragraph 3 says, "And now, at last, he had earned enough money to buy one.")

2. Why did Franco Muñoz offer to give Armando a home? (Franco was impressed by Armando's resolute spirit and felt compassion for him. He and his wife had no son of their own.)

3. What did Armando like about his life with the Muñozes? What did he not like? (He liked living in the country. He disliked the life of schedule, with regular meals, work hours, and school hours.)

4. Armando missed how many days of school? (one)

5. What are the evidences that he was truly sorry? (He bought a lovely pen for the teacher. He used his money to buy this instead of the pocketknife he wanted so much.)

6. Why can you trust adults when Armando could not? (Our relationships with adults have been good, whereas Armando's were poor.)

26. This story has an excellent opening paragraph. It catches the reader's attention by raising questions in his mind. One such question is, "Why is Armando hiding?" Write two other questions that the opening paragraph might raise in the reader's mind. **(Sample questions.)**

     What had happened in the classroom? Why was the teacher anxious? Why doesn't Armando want to return to the classroom?

C. Writing for Comprehension

27. What is the main lesson of the two-sided coin? Answer in one or two sentences.

     Misunderstandings often have more than one side.

     We should try to see the other person's side of the issue also.

28. Write several sentences that tell how the story might have ended if Brother Montealegre and the Muñozes had been harsh and angry with Armando.

     (Sentences could say that Armando might never have returned and might later have become a criminal.)

D. Review

29. The person who tells a story is called the ___narrator.___.

30. Seeing in our minds the events and scenes in a story is called ___visualizing.___.

31. Write whether each sentence is true (**T**) or false (**F**).

     _F_ a. A skiff is a small wagon.

     _T_ b. Something unwieldy is cumbersome.

     _T_ c. Something infinite is boundless or everlasting.

Fifth Reader Workbook

 21. Growing Smiles

A smile is an expression of friendliness that can be understood in any language. Generally, when you give a smile, you gain a smile. Having a cheerful smile is a good habit that we should practice.

A. Defining for Comprehension

1. Some English words look so nearly alike that we can easily confuse them. The word **quite** in the first line of the poem looks similar to **quit** and **quiet.** On the lines below, write the phonetic spelling and the definition for each of these words.

    a. quite ___(kwīt), completely; entirely; truly___

    b. quit ___(kwĭt), stop doing something; cease___

    c. quiet ___(kwī´ ĭt), not making noise; still___

2. In the second line of the poem, is the word **wrinkles** a noun or a verb? ___verb___

3. Copy one compound word from stanza 3 and one from stanza 4.

    ___someone___   ___everywhere___

B. Reading for Comprehension

4. This poem has a good pattern of *rhyme.* Look at the last word in each line, and write the two from each stanza that rhyme.

    (1) ___face, place___

    (2) ___do, two___

    (3) ___back, track___

    (4) ___care, everywhere___

5. What unpleasant expression wrinkles up your face more than a smile does? ___frown___

6. According to one stanza, smiles multiply so fast that it is hard to count them all. Which stanza suggests that?

    ___third___

7. A smile is like light: it cannot be stored. As soon as a person stops smiling, the smile is gone. Write the two lines that suggest this idea.

    ___And when it's gone, you never find___

    ___Its secret hiding place.___

8. Write the line from the fourth stanza that suggests that smiles are not limited to one language or people.

    ___That smiles go everywhere.___

54

Lesson 21

To the Teacher

Have the students read this poem chorally, using good expression and paying attention to the punctuation. Rhythm should serve as something "extra" in a poem, and not as the main object. If too much attention is given to rhythm, students tend to read poetry in a singsong manner.

Take time to discuss the content of the poem. Point out that smiles "grow" by being spread from one person to the next. (See Discussion Starters, number 1.) Also discuss the rhythm pattern and the rhyme pattern of the poem.

In preparation for exercise 10, you may want to compose a few lines of poetry on the board. Encourage the faster students to write a second stanza. Teacher involvement in exercise 10 is vital if the pupils are to get a good start.

Literary concept in this lesson:

Rhyme (See exercise 4.)
Rhythm (See exercise 9.)

Discussion Starters

1. If you smile at five people today and each of them smiles at five others because of it, how many people would have smiled? (thirty-one people, if each person smiles back)

2. In the first line, does *funny* mean "strange" or "something that makes you laugh"? (strange)

3. Should you smile even when you do not feel like it? (Yes,

C. Writing for Comprehension

9. This poem has a simple kind of *rhythm.* It has a regular pattern of accented and unaccented syllables. Below is the first line of the poem divided into syllables and marked to show the accent pattern. Mark the syllables of the other three lines in the same way.

⌣ / ⌣ / ⌣ / ⌣ /
A smile is quite a fun-ny thing—
   ⌣ / ⌣ / ⌣ /
It wrin-kles up your face,
   ⌣ / ⌣ / ⌣ / ⌣ /
And when it's gone, you nev-er find
   ⌣ / ⌣ / ⌣ /
Its se-cret hid-ing place.

10. After studying the rhyme and rhythm patterns of "Growing Smiles," write a stanza with four lines of your own. Try to use the same rhyme and rhythm patterns. You may want to write about singing or working, or about good friends. Perhaps you will want to write a second stanza to develop your thought more fully.

   (Teacher: You may need to help students understand the rhythm pattern, and give

   some suggestions to get them started. Check poems for consistent rhyme and

   rhythm. You may want to give extra credit for a second stanza or assign it only to

   the more capable students.)

D. Review

11. Write whether each sentence is true (**T**) or false (**F**).

   __T__   a. An urchin can be a little girl.

   __F__   b. A thoroughfare is a marketplace.

   __T__   c. An argument against something can be called an objection.

12. Write what is meant by visualizing. _____

   seeing in our minds the events or scenes in a story

in general. Often the act of smiling will help you to feel
more cheerful.)
4. We have studied one other poem that is somewhat like
this one. Which one is it? ("It's in Your Face")

Fifth Reader Workbook

 ## 22. Flat-tail: An Autumn Night in the Life of a Beaver

The beaver is another one of the marvels of God's creation. This essay shows various ways in which God equipped the beaver for life in streams and ponds. Especially interesting is the way beavers build dams, cut down trees, and store food for winter.

A. Defining for Comprehension

Match these words with their definitions. You will not use all the letters.

_b_	1. sporadic	a.	Preying animals.
_e_	2. vicinity	b.	Happening at irregular times; occasional.
_c_	3. unperturbed	c.	Not disturbed or bothered.
_h_	4. cumbersome	d.	Call for (help); enlist.
_g_	5. outstrip	e.	Nearby area; neighborhood.
_a_	6. predators	f.	Able to be molded or formed.
_d_	7. recruit	g.	Excel; exceed; go faster.
		h.	Clumsy; awkward.

Use these three words to fill in the blanks below.

amiss   meshed   resounding

8. John's account of what happened ___meshed___ well with the evidence.

9. Something is ___amiss___; my pencil isn't where I put it!

10. The ___resounding___ hoot of the owl echoed through the night.

11. Write the phonetic spelling and the definition for the word **debris.** _____
    (də·brē′), broken remains; rubbish _____

B. Reading for Comprehension

*How well did you concentrate? Circle the letter of the correct answer to question 12–19 below. If you must look back in the essay for an answer, write **X** before that question.*

12. The essay begins with part of a Bible verse from which book?

   (a.) Genesis
   b. Exodus
   c. Revelation

56

Lesson 22

To the Teacher

Discuss with the students the marvel of God's creative work as illustrated by the beaver. Tell them that beavers are native only to North America. Have them try to visualize the dam, the pond, and the creek. You may wish to find more facts about the beaver in an encyclopedia or a nature book. Show them colored pictures. Such materials will be needed for the pupils to do exercises 20 and 23.

The essay does not explain how a beaver's tail becomes "slashed and scarred from numerous battles fought with other beavers." This happens in spring soon after the beaver kits are born, when the male beavers and the yearlings wander off into the woods. They meet other beavers that are out for the same reason. Apparently because they have nothing else to do, the beavers fight among themselves, going after each other's tails in particular.

Contrast the nature of the mink and the lynx in the essay. The mink was simply a nuisance, whereas the lynx was a deadly foe. (See Discussion Starters, number 2.)

Discuss the teamwork needed for bringing trees to the pond and for building a lodge. As all the beavers worked together, communication was essential, especially in the event of possible danger.

For exercise 23, you may wish to draw a sketch on the board as you read the essay together.

Note: This essay has been significantly revised from its

13. About how much did Flat-tail weigh?

    a. six pounds   b. sixteen pounds   (c.) sixty pounds

14. What animal had taken up residence on the main dam?

    (a.) a mink   b. a muskrat   c. an otter

15. What was the main reason for the beavers' canal from the felling area to the main pond?

    a. convenience   (b.) safety   c. recreation

16. Can a beaver control the direction that a tree will fall?

    a. always   (b.) never   c. sometimes

17. Where can a beaver travel the fastest?

    a. on land   b. in a tree   (c.) in water

18. At what level were the beaver family's living quarters located?

    a. at the bottom of the pond

    b. just below the surface of the pond

    (c.) above the surface of the pond

19. Where did the beavers store their supply of food for winter?

    a. at the felling area   (b.) under the water   c. in the canal

20. Sometimes we may want to check the accuracy of what we read. This is known as ***verifying*** information. For example, the essay tells us that a beaver's teeth keep growing and that he slaps the water with his tail as a warning signal. Use an encyclopedia or a book about animals to verify this information. When you find the information, write the page number and the name of the book where you found it.

    (Individual answers.)

C. Writing for Comprehension

21. Describe Flat-tail's appearance, and tell why his tail was slashed and scarred.

    (Sample description.) Flat-tail was brown, and he had a square-cornered nose and a flat tail. His tail was slashed and scarred from battles fought with other beavers. (Older editions of the reader say his back had many scars and the end of his tail had been bitten off by another beaver.)

former version. Its title in earlier editions of the reader is "Square-tail: An Autumn Day in the Life of a Beaver." However, the workbook exercises are compatible with both the revised and the earlier editions of the reader.

Literary concept in this lesson:

Verifying (See exercise 20.)

Discussion Starters

1. What made the main dam so strong? How does a curve make a dam stronger? (The main dam was made of alternate layers of sticks, branches, logs, and mud, and it was five feet thick at the base. A curved dam is stronger than a straight one because some of the force of the water pressure is diverted to its two ends.)

2. Who are the beaver's enemies? (lynx, wolverines, and timber wolves)

3. What were Flat-tail's two main activities in the essay? (keeping the dams in good repair and gathering food for winter)

4. What was the purpose of the smaller dams and ponds below the main one? (to relieve the water pressure on the main dam)

5. How does a beaver use his hind feet and tail when swimming? (He pushes himself along with his webbed hind feet and uses his flat tail as a rudder.)

6. How did the beavers use the trails or slides on the dams? (to go from one pond to the next)

Fifth Reader Workbook

22. What different kinds of work did the beaver family do in the essay?

Flat-tail and his mate inspected the dams and repaired the main dam. The parents

and yearlings stored a winter supply of food.

_____

23. Imagine that you are hovering over Flat-tail's home in a helicopter. Draw a simple sketch of
the main pond with its lodge and the canal. Also sketch the smaller ponds with their dams.
Label the lodge, the canal, and the main dam.

    Sketch should show the ponds in proper proportion, with the lodge in

    the center of the big pond. (Older editions of the reader do not specify

    the location of the lodge.) Check labels.

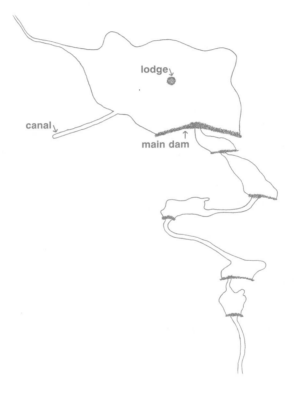

58

23. A Simple Kind of Bravery

Esther in this story wanted to be brave like her favorite Bible character. But she had to learn that true bravery is in simple, unselfish service to others and not in exalting oneself.

A. Defining for Comprehension

1. When Esther's dog began to bark, the story says that Esther was "jerked sharply from her reverie." Circle the letter of the statement below that best restates this thought.

   a. She looked up quickly.

   b. She awakened quickly from her daydream.

   c. She jumped in surprise.

Here is a list of words from the story. For each underlined word or phrase in the sentences below, write a word from this list that could be used instead.

sparse	dubiously	premeditated
ornery	drastic	reproved
ruefully	deftly	charges
heroine	forlornly	

2. Abigail is known as a <u>brave woman</u>. _____heroine_____

3. The lost duckling waddled about <u>in a sad, lonely way</u>. _____forlornly_____

4. The grass on the dry plain was <u>thinly scattered</u>. _____sparse_____

5. Mother <u>quickly and skillfully</u> folded the laundry. _____deftly_____

6. A teacher's <u>persons to be cared for</u> are his pupils. _____charges_____

7. Grandfather <u>rebuked</u> the disobedient boy. _____reproved_____

8. The weather made a <u>very great</u> change overnight. _____drastic_____

9. The boy's response had been <u>planned in advance</u>. _____premeditated_____

10. He admitted <u>regretfully</u> that he had made a mistake. _____ruefully_____

11. Father considered the matter <u>doubtfully</u>. _____dubiously_____

12. The <u>contrary</u> old mule refused to budge. _____ornery_____

B. Reading for Comprehension.

13. Why was it foolish for Esther to try proving her bravery by climbing onto the house roof? Circle the letter of the best answer.

   a. She was doing it for a selfish reason.

   b. She was a poor example to her little sisters.

   c. She did a dangerous thing that was not necessary.

   d. For all the reasons above.

Lesson 23

To the Teacher

Briefly recall the story of Queen Esther. What brave deed did she do? Discuss the meaning of bravery as Esther's mother described it—doing what has to be done and trusting God for the strength to do it, without any premeditation or desire to impress others. This describes well both Queen Esther's bravery in going to the king and Esther's bravery in helping her younger sisters and little brother at the time of the fire.

Have the students find picturesque verbs and adjectives that describe how people acted or felt at different points in the story. As they read orally, be sure they read with expression, especially where there is conversation.

The word *daudyhouse* (dô′ dē hous) comes from a German compound that means "grandpa house." It refers to the addition to the main house (or small house located near the main house) that many Amish and Mennonite people build for their elderly parents.

Contrast Esther's behavior in the first part of the story with her behavior during the fire. In both instances she was being brave, yet there was a great difference. What was it? (In the first part she had a selfish motive, but at the time of the fire she forgot herself in her concern for others.)

Fifth Reader Workbook

14. Read Matthew 20:26, 27. What must a person be willing to do if he wants to be truly great?

    He must be willing to serve.

15. Writers do not always include details in a story that we can easily understand from what they do tell us. The story says that Eva disappeared as Esther prepared to climb onto the house roof. According to what we read soon afterward, what was Eva's purpose for leaving?

    Eva went to tell Mother what Esther was doing.

16. What was another foolish thing that Esther had done earlier to try to prove her bravery?

    She had tried to ride some calves.

17. Why does the story title call Esther's bravery a simple kind? Circle the letter of the best answer.

    (a.) She simply did what was needed at the moment.

    b. She tried to prove herself brave by keeping the children.

    c. Her brave deeds were not as important as those done by Esther in the Bible.

18. At the end of the story, Mother and Esther shared a secret smile because

    a. Esther had acted like a mature person.

    b. They were glad that the fire was not worse.

    (c.) Esther had learned what true bravery is.

C. Writing for Comprehension

19. Sometimes true bravery means giving up something that we would like to have or do. Tell what Esther sacrificed as part of her bravery.

    Esther gave up seeing all the excitement and what was happening to the house.

20. To be brave and act wisely, we need to think clearly rather than panic. In the second part of the story, find at least three examples of clear thinking on Esther's part. (Sample answers.)

    She did not jump out the second-story window.

    She took the children to the car to keep them warm.

    She opened the car window a crack. She prepared a bottle for the baby.

    She did not leave the children alone in the car any longer than necessary.

60

Discussion Starters

1. Esther is a brave Bible character mentioned in this story. Name some others. What shows their bravery? (Examples will vary. Their bravery is shown in that they did what needed to be done, regardless of how they may have felt.)

2. Was Jehu brave because he drove "furiously"? (No. He may have done it as a show of "manliness.")

3. Did the little girls understand bravery? How do you know? (They had a faulty understanding of bravery at the beginning of the story, but it was influenced by Esther's actions. By the end of the story, the little girls' understanding of bravery was closer to Mother's idea.)

4. Mother felt that Esther was brave already at the beginning of the story. Why did she think so? (Esther stayed in the house alone to watch her little brother. She had gone out in the dark to look for Blondie.)

5. What did Mother mean when she said, "Brave deeds are not premeditated"? (She meant that brave deeds are not planned ahead of time. They are done when special needs arise, and such needs usually cannot be predicted.)

6. The story does not say that Mother ever checked on the children in the car. What does that tell you? (Mother considered Esther trustworthy.)

7. What day of the week was it when the fire started? (Sunday)

D. Review

*Write whether each sentence is true (**T**) or false (**F**).*

F 21. To verify means to concentrate on a story for details.

T 22. An opening paragraph may catch a reader's interest by raising questions in his mind or suggesting that something exciting is about to happen.

F 23. To visualize means to draw a picture of something in a story.

T 24. Rhyme and rhythm patterns are part of poetry.

T 25. A narrator is a person who tells a story.

F 26. The main character in "A Simple Kind of Bravery" is Esther's mother.

Lesson 24

To the Teacher

Discuss the fact that God is truly the source of all that we have, and specifically of our daily bread. He makes it possible for us to enjoy our daily bread. You might refer to several Scriptures that bring this out, such as Isaiah 55:10 and James 1:17.

Discuss the phrase "back of" as explained in the workbook. (A poet's departure from established rules is called poetic license.) Below are two stanzas from another poem with the "back of" theme; this poem was written in about the same period as the one in today's lesson. In fact, since "The Thinker" applauds the powers of man and gives no credit to God, it may be what prompted Maltbie D. Babcock

(a minister) to write "Our Daily Bread."

Be sure the students understand that an essay is composed of three parts—introduction, body, and conclusion. Explain what is included in each of these parts. In a longer composition, the introduction and the conclusion are usually a full paragraph. But in a three-paragraph essay, the first and the last sentences are sufficient for the introduction and the conclusion.

Stress the fact that the quantity of words is not as important as their quality. It is better to say much in few words than to say little in many words. Worthwhile thoughts, clearly worded sentences, and neat writing should be our goal.

Be sure the students understand the sequence of thought in the poem: sun, rain, wheat, mill, flour, bread.

Encourage the students to rewrite their compositions until

Fifth Reader Workbook

 ## 24. Our Daily Bread

The poem "Our Daily Bread" reminds us that God is the Author of all good things. James 1:17 says, "Every good gift and every perfect gift is from above, and cometh down from the Father of lights, with whom is no variableness, neither shadow of turning." This poem is in line with that Bible verse.

Note: You may know the English rule that says it is incorrect to use "in back of" for "behind." This poem was written around 1900, when "back of" may have been a proper expression. Also, poets sometimes make exceptions to the normal rules so that their poetic lines work out better. "Back of" produces better rhythm in this poem than "behind" would do.

Write a three-paragraph essay explaining how God, who brings showers and sunshine, is "back of" our daily bread. Use the following outline for your composition.

I. Who gives us our daily bread? (Use Isaiah 55:10 in this paragraph.)

II. How does God give us our daily bread? (Use the steps given in the poem.)

III. How can we thank God for our daily bread?

Remember that your opening paragraph should introduce your subject in an interesting way. Then you should present the main body of your thoughts in a number of clear, well-written sentences. In the final paragraph, conclude your thoughts with one or two brief sentences. Review the Keys to Good Writing in Lesson 12 before you begin.

Review for Test 4

1. Be sure you know the meanings of the vocabulary words in Lessons 19–24.

2. Be sure you know what these terms mean. The last two are from earlier lessons.

narrator (Lesson 19)

visualizing (Lesson 19)

rhyme and rhythm patterns (Lesson 21)

verifying (Lesson 22)

main idea (Lesson 2)

opening paragraph (Lessons 16, 20)

they are the very best that they can do. Grade the compositions primarily for content, but also for grammar and neatness.

"Our Daily Bread" would be easy to illustrate in an art class. You may wish to write the poem on a poster and allow space around it for the student's drawings.

The Thinker

Back of the beating hammer
By which the steel is wrought,
Back of the workshop's clamor
The seeker may find the thought—
The thought that is ever master
Of iron and steam and steel,
That rises above disaster
And tramples it under heel!

Back of the motors humming,
Back of the bells that sing,
Back of the hammers drumming,
Back of the cranes that swing,
There is the eye which scans them
Watching through stress and strain,
There is the mind which plans them—
Back of the brawn, the brain!

—*Berton Braley*

25. The Rescue

This is a story of true bravery, a heartwarming account of a father's love in action. The story contains a good bit of suspense. Although suspense adds much interest, it is not the most important element of a story. The most important thing is the main truth or lesson that the story teaches.

A. Defining for Comprehension

This story contains a number of expressions used by sailors. Match the terms with their definitions. You should not find this hard if you study the context.

_d_	1. northeasters	a.	Man from "down east" (New England).
_l_	2. rigging	b.	Small telescope.
_g_	3. made the port	c.	Fasten; tie.
_j_	4. mate	d.	Storms or winds from the northeast.
_a_	5. down-easter	e.	Put (a boat) into water for travel.
_k_	6. tide	f.	Splashed us two times.
_b_	7. glass	g.	Reached the harbor.
_e_	8. launched	h.	Back end of a boat.
_h_	9. stern	i.	Devices for keeping oars in place.
_f_	10. washed us twice	j.	Officer second in command of a ship.
_i_	11. oarlocks	k.	Rising or falling of the ocean surface.
_c_	12. make fast	l.	Ropes and pulleys fastened to the sails of a ship.

Here is a list of words from the story. For each underlined word or phrase in the sentences below, write a word from the list that could be used instead. One word will not be used.

fortnight	exerted	tempo
aroused	enveloped	plied
vigilant	latitudes	
intensely	lethargy	

13. Toward evening the ship became <u>closed in</u> by fog.
    enveloped

14. The ship <u>made its way</u> steadily through the <u>extremely</u> cold water.
    plied, intensely

63

Lesson 25

To the Teacher

After the students have read the story silently, have them read it orally by turns. This story is excellent for oral reading because it is full of feeling and a sense of urgency. Encourage the students to read with proper expression.

Indicate the probable setting of this story on a wall map. It took place near New York City. The chunk of ice was probably floating out of Long Island Sound toward the ocean.

Help the students understand the seaman's language. Be sure they understand what is meant by the tide running out and carrying a cake of ice to the sea.

The determination and perseverance displayed by Mr.

Larkin and the captain are noteworthy. Ask the pupils what made them do it. Ask the pupils if the bravery expressed in this story meets the qualifications of true bravery.

Discuss the final paragraph with the students. Point out how different the ending would have been if Mr. Larkin had done nothing when he thought he saw a child on the ice, and would have learned afterward that two children had floated out to sea and perished. Ask the pupils what Mr. Larkin meant when he said, "But very easy here." (He felt at peace in his heart.)

Be sure to discuss at least several of the words in the second group of exercises in Part A.

Fifth Reader Workbook

15. We sang the song at a faster <u>speed</u> in the chorus.

    tempo

16. The men <u>put forth</u> great effort to stay awake, but <u>the drowsiness of a person freezing to death</u> soon overtook them.

    exerted, lethargy

17. The captain <u>awakened</u> the men and urged them to remain <u>watchful</u>.

    aroused, vigilant

18. Our family was away from home for a <u>period of two weeks</u>.

    fortnight

B. Reading for Comprehension

19. *Suspense* is uncertainty on the reader's part about what will happen in a story. Often it results when the main character is in great danger or difficulty. Then the reader wants to read on to find out what happened.

    What is the main cause of suspense in "The Rescue"? Circle the letter of the correct answer.

    a. We are not sure whether the sailors will earn an extra month's wages.
    b. We are not sure whether the men will reach the cake of ice and rescue the children.
    c. We are not sure why the children are on the cake of ice.

20. What is meant by the phrase "with no little difficulty"? Circle the letter of the best answer.

    a. without difficulty   b. with slight difficulty   c. with great difficulty

21. The *plot* of a story is the pattern of events in the story. If you were to list the main events of a story in the order they occurred, you would be writing an outline of the story plot.

    Below is a partial outline of the plot of "The Rescue." Complete it by filling in main events that occurred between the ones given.

    a. Mr. Larkin sighted the children.
    b. Mr. Larkin awoke the captain.
    c. The cutter was launched.
    d. The crew members gave out.
    e. The captain and Mr. Larkin began rowing.
    f. The children were reached and rescued.

64

Literary concepts in this lesson:

Suspense (Discuss exercise 19 in class.)
Plot of a story (Discuss exercise 21 in class.)

Discussion Starters

1. Why could the men not see the children clearly at first? (The moon was behind a cloud.)
2. What did the captain and Mr. Larkin promise the men if they would bring the boat to the cake of ice? (The captain promised a month's extra wages. Mr. Larkin promised another month's pay.)
3. How do you know that Mr. Larkin cared about his men? (He told them to lie down while he and the captain rowed.)
4. What terrible thought nearly made the narrator's heart stop beating? (the thought that Mr. Larkin had become too tired to keep rowing)
5. How did the men get the children warm as quickly as possible? (They took off the children's jackets and shoes, and held the children in contact with their own warm bodies.)
6. How old do you think the boys were? (They were old enough to be out playing alone, but small enough to be held inside the men's overcoats. This suggests an age of six to eight years.)

C. Writing for Comprehension

22. One sentence says that the rescue boat "made little more headway than the tide." What does this phrase mean?

     The rescue boat did not go much faster than the tide was going out.

23. Both Mr. Larkin and the captain had a "father's heart." What did this have to do with their efforts to rescue the children?

     They had a father's love for children, which made them do all they could to rescue the boys.

24. Explain Mr. Larkin's statement in the last paragraph of the story.

     Mr. Larkin's arms were sore from the hard rowing, but his heart was at peace because the boys had been rescued.

D. Review

25. Who is the narrator of this story, Mr. Larkin or the captain?   the captain

26. What do we mean by verifying?

     checking the accuracy of what we read (by using other books)

Lesson 26

To the Teacher

This story is based on an account in the *Martyrs Mirror* (page 428). The account is in the part of the book that deals with Christian martyrs of 1528. Show on a map where the story took place. Moravia is a region in the eastern part of the Czech Republic.

Before reading the story together, give the pupils sufficient background information so that they can understand and appreciate it. Discuss the basic beliefs of the Anabaptists, how the state churches in various European countries did not tolerate those beliefs, and how the Anabaptists were persecuted by the state churches as they stood true to their faith.

Fifth Reader Workbook

 ## 26. Hands That Shed Innocent Blood

God sometimes chooses to deliver His people from persecution as he did Daniel from the lion's den. At other times He takes His persecuted servants home to Himself through death as He did John the Baptist. This story from the *Martyrs Mirror* also shows that God sometimes punishes the persecutors themselves. God always knows what is best.

A. Defining for Comprehension

Here is a list of words from the story. After each word or phrase below, write a word from the list that is opposite or nearly opposite in meaning. You will not use all the words.

menacingly   apprehending   oppressor
witnessed   commotion   heresy
pious   aroused   scoundrels
impractical   bailiff

1. sound doctrine __heresy__
2. releasing __apprehending__
3. prisoner __bailiff__
4. upright men __scoundrels__
5. helper __oppressor__
6. stillness __commotion__
7. workable __impractical__
8. subdued __aroused__
9. comfortingly __menacingly__
10. overlooked __witnessed__

11. The story uses the verbs "demanded," "thundered," "snapped," and "shouted" to tell how Judge Louis spoke to the council. It also tells us that he had "bejeweled hands." Consider what these words tell us about Judge Louis. Then circle the letter of each word or phrase below that is a fitting description of Judge Louis.

    (a.) ungodly
    (b.) cruel
    c. considerate
    (d.) hot-tempered
    (e.) proud
    (f.) impatient
    g. happy
    h. grateful

B. Reading for Comprehension

12. The title of this story is based on Proverbs 6:17. "Hands that shed innocent blood" is one of the things the Lord hates.

    a. Read Matthew 27:3, 4. Who confessed to having shed innocent blood in these verses?

    __Judas Iscariot__

    b. Whose blood was that man responsible for? __Jesus' blood__

66

This story provides an excellent opportunity to help the students think about the significance of what they read. We sometimes call this "reading between the lines." For example, the first several paragraphs contain a number of picturesque descriptions that give us insight into the character of the judge: "bejeweled hands"; "leaned across the council table"; "small, glittering eyes"; "glaring menacingly"; "demanded"; "thundered impatiently"; "snapped"; and "rose slightly in his chair." Discuss the significance of these expressions. (See Discussion Starters, number 1.)

The story gives a picture of the carefulness but increasing boldness of Balthazar. Discuss his statements about the Anabaptists. Did he fully defend them? (See Discussion Starters, number 4.) What is meant by the statement that the

councilors sought to wash their hands of innocent blood? (They tried to relieve themselves of their responsibility.)

Is there any significance in the fact that the oldest man spoke first, followed by a large man? (See Discussion Starters, number 3.) Point out the change this made in the other councilors, from "squirmed uneasily" and "remained strangely silent" to "The councilors were not intimidated. They stared stubbornly at the table top."

Discuss the significance of the way the story ends. Do not leave the impression that God always punishes evildoers in this manner. Rather, point out that "all things work together for good to them that love God." This applies to the martyred Anabaptist in the story as well as those who escaped from the meeting.

13. Notice the councilors' actions in paragraph 3. What was the reason for these actions?
    They dared not meet the judge's gaze.

14. What three things did Judge Louis accuse the Anabaptists of?
    not attending church, not confessing to the priest, not having their infants baptized

15. What is a traitor?   one who betrays his friend or his country

16. Why did not many townspeople witness the execution of the five Anabaptists?
    The people were sympathetic to the Anabaptists.

C. Writing for Comprehension

17. Write a paragraph describing what happened to Judge Louis when he tried to apprehend the Anabaptists who were having a meeting.
    (Paragraph should mention how and where he fell, how he responded, and how he
    suffered and died.)

18. Many of the people believed that Judge Louis suffered and died as a judgment from God. What evidence shows that Judge Louis may have realized this himself?
    In his suffering, Judge Louis said over and over, "Oh, the Baptists, the Baptists!"

19. Why is the Bible verse (Jeremiah 22:3) a fitting way to end the story?
    The verse is a command to do no violence and shed no innocent blood.
    Judge Louis was guilty of these things and suffered God's judgment for it.

D. Review

20. Find the paragraph that begins with the words, "Realizing that his threatened trip." Copy a simile that is used in this paragraph.   like a caged lion

21. Which is more important, the suspense or the lesson in a story?   the lesson

22. What word is used for the pattern of events in a story?   plot

Discussion Starters

1. What kind of man was Judge Louis? What are bejeweled hands? (The judge was a domineering, impatient, hot-tempered man. Bejeweled hands are hands with many jeweled rings on the fingers.)

2. At the beginning of the story, why were the ten councilors squirming? (because of Judge Louis's threatening manner)

3. Why do you think Balthazar spoke first? (He was the oldest and most experienced.)

4. What approving and disapproving things did Balthazar say about the Anabaptists? (Approving: They were kind and generous neighbors. They had done no harm to anyone. Disapproving: They held strange beliefs. They read the Bible at home instead of attending the state church, which Balthazar said was foolish.)

5. Why were the people slow to give him information about the Anabaptists? (They were sympathetic with the Anabaptists.)

6. What is a town loafer? Why do you think he was the one who gave the information? (A town loafer is a person who loafs about in town and does little work. He did it to get easy money.)

Fifth Reader Workbook

 27. I Paused Last Eve

Unbelieving men have tried for centuries to destroy the Bible, but it has always withstood their attacks. There is only one reason for the endurance of this Book: it is God's Word. Man's efforts to destroy truth will always be useless.

A. Defining for Comprehension

Write a word from the poem for each definition below.

1. Another word for **evening**. _____eve_____

2. Object giving a bell-like sound when struck. ___chime___

3. Beat with successive strokes. _____batter_____

4. Forceful strokes. _____blows_____

5. Heavy steel block for shaping metal objects. __anvil__

Circle the letter of the best answer in each exercise.

6. **Vesper** refers to evening. What then is the "vesper's chime"?

   (a.) the ringing of the blacksmith's hammer in the evening

   b. the sound of the blacksmith's song in the evening

   c. the sound of hammers falling to the floor in the evening

7. A skeptic is a person who

   a. hates.   (b.) doubts.   c. believes.

B. Reading for Comprehension

8. Line 9 of the poem refers to "the anvil of God's Word." This is a good example of a figure of speech. It is much like saying, "The anvil is God's Word."

   Is this figure of speech a simile or a metaphor? __metaphor__

9. Instead of making a comparison that describes just one detail, the author based the whole poem on this figure of speech. He used several facts about actual objects to help the reader understand the truths that he was presenting. (Teacher: This is called an extended metaphor.)

   Fill in the blanks in the following sentences to explain the meaning of the comparison.

   a. God's ___Word___ is compared to an ___anvil___.

   b. The opposition of ___skeptics___ is compared to ___hammers___ beating upon the anvil.

68

Lesson 27

To the Teacher

Assign this poem to be read silently by the students. When they have finished, demonstrate the use of a conversational tone when reading the dialogue between the author and the blacksmith. Then ask one of the pupils to read the poem orally.

Point out the deep meaning that lies in this poem. Be sure the students understand the comparison between the anvil and the Bible, and between the hammers and the skeptics' blows. Regardless of how long or how hard the skeptics' blows fall upon the Bible, it remains unchanged and unchangeable. God has said that His Word shall stand forever.

You may want to mention that in Europe during the 1700s, the French atheist Voltaire stated that the Bible would be obsolete within a hundred years. Soon after his death, Voltaire's house was purchased by a Bible society and used for the publication and distribution of God's Word.

You will need to gather some facts about blacksmiths in preparation for exercise 13. Present it to the class in lecture form, and have them take notes on the information.

Literary concept in this lesson:

Taking notes (See exercise 13.)

Circle the letter of the best answer in each exercise.

10. The "noise of falling blows" is a comparison that refers to

    a. the way a blacksmith hits the anvil.

    (b.) the arguments and reasoning of the skeptics.

    c. the way the Bible disproves the skeptics.

11. What is the main idea or lesson of this poem?

    a. Hammers wear out before anvils.

    b. Many skeptics have tried to destroy the Bible.

    (c.) God's Word remains unchanged regardless of all the efforts to destroy it.

C. Writing for Comprehension

12. Finish the question that the author asked the blacksmith.

"Since you have so many battered hammers, how many __anvils do you have__?"

13. At one time there were blacksmith shops in nearly all villages. They are not so common today. Your teacher will give you some information about blacksmiths. As he talks, write down the main points. This is called **taking notes.**

    Use your notes to write a paragraph about blacksmiths.

__(Paragraph should be written in student's own words according to information__
__provided by the teacher.)__

D. Review

*Write whether each sentence is true (**T**) or false (**F**).*

_F_ 14. A bailiff is a prisoner.

_T_ 15. Oarlocks are part of rowboats.

_F_ 16. The pattern of events in a story is called suspense.

_T_ 17. Something that is not workable is impractical.

_T_ 18. Heresy is the opposite of sound doctrine.

Discussion Starters

1. Why do you think the blacksmith had a twinkling eye when he answered the question? (He thought the poet surely knew the answer.)
2. In what ways does the anvil, God's Word, never change? (Its teachings are always the same, regardless of the way people's ideas may change.)
3. Can you think of some ways in which people have tried to destroy God's Word? (In Old Testament times, King Jehoiakim burned Jeremiah's scroll. In the Middle Ages, church officials tried to destroy Bible translations such as the one made by William Tyndale. In modern times, communist rulers try to destroy people's Bibles. Also, many scholars have tried to discredit the Bible by saying it contains errors or that it is out of date.)

Fifth Reader Workbook

28. Salmon Days

It is interesting to see how this family worked together to prepare their winter's supply of fish. The father's job at the sawmill must also have been important, and it was not customary for the men to help with the fishing. We can each help with our family's work just as Emma and her brothers did.

A. Defining for Comprehension

*Write one of these words from the story to complete each sentence below. (The first two are from the introduction.) In the blank before each sentence, write whether the word you chose is a noun (**n.**), a verb (**v.**), an adjective (**adj.**), or an adverb (**adv.**).*

hordes	buoy	entrails
spawn	precariously	plummets
aroma	extract	
oblong	performance	

_n._ 1. The kitchen was filled with the delicious ____aroma____ of fresh bread.

adv. 2. The lamp tottered ____precariously____ and then fell with a crash.

_n._ 3. Jake was impressed with the tractor's ____performance____ on the steep hillside.

_v._ 4. The beekeeper will ____extract____ the honey from the honeycomb.

_n._ 5. Sometimes crops have been destroyed by ____hordes____ of grasshoppers.

_n._ 6. After butchering the chickens, we buried the ____entrails____ behind the barn.

adj. 7. Because of its ____oblong____ shape, the ball did not fly straight.

_v._ 8. Salmon will ____spawn____ in the same stream where they hatched.

_n._ 9. A ____buoy____ showed where hidden rocks lay under the water.

_v._ 10. An eagle ____plummets____ to the ground to capture its prey.

11. Write the phonetic spelling and the meaning of **cache.** _____

(kăsh), a place for hiding or storing supplies _____

70

Lesson 28

To the Teacher

Locate British Columbia on a wall map. If the students are unfamiliar with the habits of salmon, you may wish to give them some background information. Tell them that salmon hatch in quiet streams in the Pacific Northwest, and then they swim downstream into the Pacific Ocean. After three years, their God-given instinct directs them to return upstream to their birthplace, where they lay their eggs and die. It is during their upstream journey that the salmon are caught and smoked or dried.

Note that the story is written in the present tense. This makes it even easier for the reader to picture the events in his mind.

Draw a sketch of a gill net on the board.

Have the students tell about family projects, such as butchering or canning, which are as exciting to them as fishing was to Emma. (See Discussion Starters, number 6.)

You will probably need to help them with the parts of speech in Part A. Check reference sources before assigning exercise 20.

Literary concept in this lesson:

Research (See exercise 20.)

B. Reading for Comprehension

12. After the salmon were netted, there were four main steps in preparing them to be stored in the wooden fish cache. List those steps. The first one is done for you.

    a.   The heads of the fish were cut off, and the fish were cleaned.

    b.   The fish were strung up to dry.

    c.   The bones were removed from the fish.

    d.   The fish were smoked.

13. Why could Mother throw out the net better than the children? Circle the letter of the best answer.

    a. Mother's fingers were more slender.

    (b.) Mother had more experience with throwing out the net.

    c. The children were not willing to learn.

14. Emma's family used a "gill net" to catch salmon. What does this tell us about how the salmon were held in the net?   The salmon were held by their gills.

15. A scavenger is an animal that eats dead animals or animal parts. Sea gulls have been called scavengers of the sea. How do the gulls live up to that name in this story?

    The gulls ate the scraps left from cleaning the fish.

16. Smoking the salmon helped to preserve them. What was another benefit of smoking the salmon? Consider especially the last paragraph of Part I.

    Smoking the salmon added a good flavor.

17. How many fish did Mother want to smoke that summer? one thousand

18. Consider how many fish the family caught in one day. At the same rate, how long would it take to catch all the salmon Mother wanted that summer? Circle the letter of the best answer.

    a. about one week   (b.) about two weeks   c. at least two months

19. Circle the letter of the phrase that best gives the main idea for each part of the story.

    Part I   **Part II**   **Part III**

    a. Setting the net   (d.) Cleaning the fish   g. Complaining about the fish

    b. Drawing in the net   e. Feeding the gulls   (h.) Preparing the fish for smoking

    (c.) Catching the fish   f. Washing the net   i. Building a smoky fire

Discussion Starters

1. What are some ways in which your family works together to prepare food for the winter? (Answers will vary.)
2. What clue near the beginning of the story tells you that this area is cool even in summer? (Mary's burrowing deeper under the quilt)
3. How did the net stay in the right position? (Floating buoys supported the upper edge, and stones weighted down the bottom edge.)
4. In what two ways did they use the lake in Part II? (for soaking the fish and washing the net)
5. Give some words that describe Emma. What was she like? (She was ambitious; she wanted to be the first one out to the lake. She showed determination in carrying the clumsy tub. She was playful in that she teased her brothers. She was a willing worker who tried to do her share.)
6. What details show the family members' warm feelings toward each other? (Emma was eager to go with her brothers. She teased them about forgetting the tub. The children splashed each other and shouted gaily as they washed the net. They fed the gulls together.)

C. Writing for Comprehension

20. When we read about something and want to learn more about it, we can get additional information by looking in reference books or by asking people who know. This is known as *research.* By doing research, we can gain a better understanding of what we read and find information that we might not discover otherwise.

    Below the entry word **fish** in an encyclopedia, look for a part called "Migration." Write a paragraph to tell what additional information you find about fish migration.

    (Paragraph should state the additional information, using the pupil's own words.)

    _____

    _____

    _____

    _____

21. In your own words, tell why it was better for Emma's family to catch the salmon they wanted early in the season.

    The early salmon had good meat because they were strong and energetic.

    The later ones would be weaker and their meat would not be as good.

    _____

    _____

29. Susan's Temptation

In this story, Susan was tempted to keep some money that did not belong to her. After all, the money would have bought some things that her family urgently needed. But there is never a right reason to do wrong. The teaching of concerned parents is a great help in overcoming a strong temptation.

A. Defining for Comprehension

1. In the first paragraph of the story, is the word **request** a noun or a verb?   <u>noun</u>

2. Find a synonym for **anger** in the first paragraph.   <u>rage</u>

3. Find a word in the second paragraph that means "two times," and a word in the third paragraph that means "two things."   <u>twice, pair</u>

4. Find a word in the story that means "arm or leg."   <u>limb</u>

5. Write a definition for each of the following words from the story. Notice how they are used in the story. You may use a dictionary.

   a. temptation   <u>something that entices a person to do wrong</u>

   b. blushed   <u>became red in the face because of shame</u>

   c. course   <u>way of doing; path along which something moves</u>

B. Reading for Comprehension

6. What kind of work did Susan's mother do for Farmer Thompson? _____
   <u>She did washing for Farmer Thompson's boarders.</u>

7. What is meant by the sentence, "It seemed the balance was tipped in favor of the comforts"? Circle the letter of the best answer.

   (a.) Susan was almost ready to keep the money because of the good things it would buy.

   b. Susan decided it would be more comfortable to her conscience if she returned the money.

8. The Golden Rule is quoted in the story. "Whatsoever ye would that men should do to you, do ye even so to them" (Matthew 7:12). How did Susan obey this verse?
   <u>She returned the money as she would want another person to return it to her if she</u>
   <u>had given him too much.</u>

9. The story suggests but does not directly say that Susan's mother was a widow. Circle the letters of the facts below that help to give this impression.

   (a.) No mention is made of Susan's father in the story.

   b. Farmer Thompson was angry with some horse dealers.

   (c.) Her mother did outside work to support the family.

   (d.) Susan thought of buying things for her mother but not her father.

   e. Susan was a sensitive girl.

73

Lesson 29

To the Teacher

Before reading this story, discuss with the students the meaning of the Golden Rule. Tell them that in today's story, remembering the Golden Rule helped someone make a right decision.

Bring in the fact that Susan had a very unselfish reason for wanting to keep the money, yet she resisted the temptation because the money did not belong to her.

Also comment on Susan's courage. It would have been difficult enough to face a kind, friendly man, but Farmer Thompson had already been in a rage the first time she was there.

Where is the turning point in Susan's struggle? What brings it about? (Seeing the garden seat reminded Susan of the truth her mother had taught her just the day before.)

Students will understand exercise 7 better if they know how a balance scale works.

Note: In older editions of the reader, the title of this story is "The First Temptation."

Discussion Starters

1. What did Mary need so that she could go to Sunday school with Susan? (a cloak for winter)

2. What good things did Susan think she could use the money for? (a cloak for her mother and shoes for her brother)

Fifth Reader Workbook

10. Below are some sentences from the story that tell us different things about Susan. After studying the paragraph where each one is found, underline the two adjectives that describe Susan's behavior as suggested by that sentence.

   a. Glad to escape so easily, Susan hurried through the gate.

      impatient, clever, <u>timid,</u> cowardly, <u>relieved</u>

   b. Startled, as if a trumpet had sounded in her ears, Susan turned suddenly around.

      <u>conscientious,</u> jumpy, confused, <u>sensitive,</u> terrified

   c. "Sir, you paid me two bills instead of one."

      bold, scornful, <u>honest,</u> defiant, <u>respectful</u>

   d. "No, sir, I thank you," she sobbed. "I do not want to be paid for doing right."

      insulted, rash, <u>upright,</u> <u>sincere,</u> careless

11. At the beginning of the story, Farmer Thompson was "in a terrible rage" at some horse dealers. At the end of the story he was quoting a Bible verse. What does this suggest about Farmer Thompson? Circle the letter of the best answer.

   a. He always tried to do what was right.

   b. He thought it was all right to get angry with some people but not with others.

   c. He probably did not live according to the truth that he knew.

C. Writing for Comprehension

12. Tell what the garden seat had to do with Susan's decision to return the money.

   The garden seat reminded Susan of what her mother had taught her.

   This helped her make the decision to return the money.

D. Review

13. What are two benefits of research?

   It gives us a better understanding of what we read.

   It gives additional information that we may not find otherwise.

74

3. Where on the way home did Susan decide to go back? (at the bridge near her home)
4. What comparison describes how startled Susan was when she thought of the Golden Rule? What comparison describes her action? What does this tell you about her? ("as if a trumpet had sounded in her ears"; "as though flying from some unseen peril"; she was afraid of doing wrong)
5. In what two ways did Farmer Thompson find fault with Susan? (He asked her why she had not come back sooner, and he accused her of planning to keep the extra money.)

6. Why do you think Susan cried? (She felt hurt by Farmer Thompson's words. It was hard to give up the extra money when it could have helped her family so much.)
7. What did Farmer Thompson mean by the verse he quoted to himself? (Mary was little but very wise.)

30. Our Refuge and Strength

This psalm is another excellent example of Hebrew poetry with parallel lines and "rhyming thoughts." It has a lofty message. God is well able to care for those who call upon Him in truth.

A. Defining for Comprehension

1. Copy three nouns in the first stanza that are closely related in meaning.

    refuge, strength, help

2. Copy a word from Psalm 46 for each of these meanings.

    a. Protection; shelter. _____ refuge

    b. Heaving; surging. _____ swelling

    c. Dwelling places; tents. _____ tabernacles

    d. Dislocated; disturbed. _____ moved

    e. Destructions; calamities. _____ desolations

    f. Uplifted; praised. _____ exalted

3. One word used several times in this psalm is a musical direction of some kind. No one knows the exact reason for its use; but for our purpose, it may be considered to have the same effect as **Amen.** Write that word. _____ Selah

B. Reading for Comprehension

4. The second and third stanzas speak of four frightening things that do not disturb the people of God. List those things.

    the earth being moved

    the mountains being carried into the sea

    the waters of the sea roaring

    the mountains shaking with the raging of the sea

5. For each line, copy the line that is its parallel. It may come before or after the line given below.

    a. The Lord of hosts is with us;

        The God of Jacob is our refuge.

    b. He breaketh the bow,

        And cutteth the spear in sunder;

    c. I will be exalted in the earth.

        I will be exalted among the heathen,

75

Lesson 30

To the Teacher

Reading Psalm 46 chorally, as arranged in this lesson, will help to bring out the majesty and beauty of its lines. It will take some practice before the students can do this smoothly and without hesitation, but the results are well worth the effort. Once the choral reading has been well accomplished, there should be no doubt in anyone's mind that this psalm is a choice selection of poetry.

Emphasize proper expression as the students read. The solo parts especially will need to be read loudly and clearly enough for everyone to hear. Most of the psalm should be read with a joyful, triumphant tone, with the exception of the sec-

ond to the last stanza. This stanza should be read in a hushed, reverent tone.

Another worthy goal in connection with this lesson is to have each student memorize Psalm 46. If the class practices the choral reading a number of times, the pupils will have a much better chance of learning the psalm thoroughly and remembering it well.

Go beyond appreciating Psalm 46 merely for its literary merit, and point out the great truths that it contains. Perhaps you or the pupils can relate incidents from your own experiences when God was "a very present help in trouble." Was there ever a time in your life when the very mountains seemed about to move out of their places? It is at such times that we really learn to appreciate the Lord for the

Fifth Reader Workbook

6. Two stanzas in Psalm 46 have identical words and may be considered the chorus of this psalm. Copy those words.

The LORD of hosts is with us.

The God of Jacob is our refuge. Selah.

C. Writing for Comprehension

7. The second to last stanza suggests the attitude that we should have as we consider the truths of this psalm. Describe that attitude in your own words.   (Sample answer.)

We should have an attitude of deep reverence for God.

8. This psalm speaks of waters roaring, mountains shaking, and the earth melting. This refers to God's power over the natural world. The psalm also speaks of the bow, the spear, and the chariot. These words suggest God's power over what?

These words suggest God's power over the military might of the nations.

D. Review for Test 5

9. Be sure you know the meanings of the vocabulary words in Lessons 25–30.

10. Be sure you know what these terms mean. The last one is from earlier lessons.

suspense (Lesson 25)
plot (Lesson 25)
taking notes (Lesson 27)
research (Lesson 28)
figures of speech (Lessons 7, 27)

76

loving, eternal, and unchanging God that He is.

Discussion Starters

1. We always need God. What are some times that we seem to especially need Him? (in times of sickness, accident, disaster, or death)
2. What is so wonderful about the fact that God never changes? (We can depend on Him regardless of how greatly things may change on the earth.)
3. What is meant by "the LORD of hosts"? (the God of the hosts of angels in heaven)
4. Who is "her" in this psalm? (the city of God, referring to Jerusalem and today to the church)
5. Why do we need to "be still" to learn about God? (We can learn the truth about God only in the absence of the noise and distractions of this world.)

31. A Mother Bear Story

Think about how a mother bear knows just when and how to prepare for her winter's sleep, and where and how to make her den. This is another example of the way God cares for His creatures through instinct, that sense of knowing how to do things without being taught. Surely God is a God of wisdom.

A. Defining for Comprehension

Write the letter of the matching definition before each word. If you need help with a word, see how it is used in the story. Each group has one definition that you will not use.

c 1. erect   a. Bodies of dead animals.
f 2. succulent   b. Hidden away.
a 3. carcasses   c. Upright; raised.
b 4. secluded   d. Confusion; disorder.
g 5. quest   e. Ask; inquire.
h 6. conifer   f. Juicy and tasty.
d 7. havoc   g. Search; pursuit.
   h. Evergreen tree.

j 8. accommodate   i. Very interesting; fascinating.
o 9. contrast   j. Have room for.
n 10. inhospitable   k. Act of watching closely.
p 11. abundant   l. Like a hospital.
m 12. cascade   m. Flow swiftly as over a waterfall.
i 13. intriguing   n. Providing no shelter or comfort.
k 14. observation   o. Noticeable or marked difference.
   p. Bountiful; plenteous.

15. Why would a wary animal often rise to make a hasty survey of its surroundings? (See the second paragraph.) Be sure you understand the meaning of **wary** before answering.

A wary animal would often rise to look around because it is always on guard against danger.

77

Lesson 31

To the Teacher

Read this story aloud to your students, having them follow along in their books. Then ask the students various questions about the story to check their comprehension.

Indicate to the students how tall the bear was when it stood upright. Compare the weight of a bear with the weight of a man. Contrast the size of a newborn cub to that of a full-grown bear.

Talk about the bear's diet and the fact that it would rather eat wild animals than tame ones. Discuss the instincts God has given bears in preparing for their winter sleep. (Bears are not true hibernators.)

Pay special attention to the last two paragraphs. Impress on the pupils' minds the reason why certain precautions need to be taken around bears.

Be sure to go over the vocabulary words together and do a few of the exercises in class.

Discussion Starters

1. What kind of bear is described in this story—black, brown, or grizzly? (black)
2. How does Mother Bear destroy much more grain than she eats? (by trampling on it)
3. What are some things a bear enjoys eating? (oats in the milk stage, small animals, honey, berries, fish)
4. How does a bear's eating habits compare with those of

Fifth Reader Workbook

B. Reading for Comprehension

16. Over what period of time does this story take place? Circle the letter of the best answer.

    (a.) From late summer to the following spring.

    b. From midwinter to early summer.

    c. From spring to early winter.

17. After reading the fourth paragraph, circle the letter of the food that Mother Bear likes best. Then underline the letter of the one that she likes least.

    a. small wild animals

    (b.) honey

    c. berries

    <u>d.</u> domestic animals

18. Why did Mother Bear choose to locate her den on a north-facing slope of a mountain?

    a. This location would not be as cold.

    (b.) The snow that helped to insulate the den would not melt as quickly.

    c. This location would be better hidden in spring.

19. What advice is the author giving in the last two paragraphs? Consider especially the sentence, "We should respect the God-given instincts of bears as well as all the animals that live in our lands and forests."

    a. We must never try to feed the wild animals in parks, or they will surely attack us.

    (b.) We should realize that instinct can cause an animal to attack us even though we may not purposely try to make it angry.

    c. The wild animals that live in our lands and forests will never bother us if we respect their God-given instincts.

20. Write whether each statement is true (**T**) or false (**F**).

    <u>T</u>   a. Bears are very watchful animals.

    <u>F</u>   b. Bears are particular about what they eat.

    <u>F</u>   c. Bears often kill sheep.

    <u>T</u>   d. During the winter sleep, a bear lives on the fat stored in its body.

    <u>T</u>   e. Newborn bears are smaller than newborn humans.

    <u>F</u>   f. Mother bears are careless about their babies.

    <u>F</u>   g. We can help bears in parks by feeding them.

78

other wild animals? (Bears are omnivorous [eating plants and animals], but most other wild animals are either herbivorous [eating only plants] or carnivorous [eating only animals].)

5. Why is it so comfortably warm in the bear's den? (because of the heat from Mother Bear's body)

6. With what humanlike action does Mother Bear train her cubs? (by paddling them when necessary)

7. When is it the most dangerous to come close to Mother Bear? Why? (It is the most dangerous when she has little ones. She will attack any man or beast that she thinks may harm her babies.)

C. Writing for Comprehension

21. In your own words, describe the cubs when they were born and again when they left the den. Be sure you include details such as size and color.   (Sample answer.)

　　　When the cubs were born, they weighed hardly one pound (older editions say

　　　hardly two pounds) and had no hair. When the cubs left the den, they had black fur,

　　　were about the size of house cats, and were as playful as kittens.

　　　_____

22. The fifth paragraph has a sentence that says Mother Bear followed a salmon stream in search of the remains of salmon that had died after spawning. Verify this information by turning to Part III of "Salmon Days" (Lesson 28) and finding a sentence which suggests that salmon die after spawning. Copy that sentence.

　　　The later ones will be so weak by the time they get here that their flesh will be

　　　mushy and half rotten.

D. Review

23. We have been calling this composition a story, but is it actually a story? Circle the letter of the composition that it really is.

    a. poem
    b. story
    c. essay

Fifth Reader Workbook

 ## 32. John Maynard

A person's character is what he really is on the inside. It is often revealed by how the person responds to various situations. This story shows us the character of John Maynard, a devoted and courageous man worthy of our admiration.

A. Defining for Comprehension

Use these words from the story to complete sentences 1–3 below. You will not use all the words.

pilot	seldom	feebly
hold	abandoning	disabled
vain	response	

1. The people were __abandoning__ the building in __response__ to a fire alarm.
2. The man was __disabled__, but his labors for the Lord were not in __vain__.
3. Before beginning the voyage, the __pilot__ went down into the __hold__ to check the cargo.
4. Write a sentence of your own, using both of the leftover words in the list above.
   (Original sentence using *seldom* and *feebly*.)

5. What is meant by the sentence, "And he beached the ship"? Be sure you understand the word **beached.**
   It means that he brought the ship ashore (onto the beach).

6. The word **aye** may be pronounced as a long **a** (Ā) or a long **i** (Ī).
   a. Which pronunciation is used when the word means "yes"? long i
   b. Which is used when the word means "ever; always"? long a

B. Reading for Comprehension

7. Since John Maynard was a pilot on a steamboat running between Detroit, Michigan, and Buffalo, New York, what lake did he navigate? You may use a map of the Great Lakes in an atlas or encyclopedia for help. Lake Erie

8. Circle the letters of the three facts below which give evidence that the story took place more than ten years ago.
   a. The pilot's name was John Maynard.
   b. John Maynard was an honest man.
   (c.) John Maynard piloted a steam-powered boat.
   (d.) They used buckets of water to try to extinguish the fire.
   e. The ship could not be saved.
   (f.) The ship could travel only 7 miles in 45 minutes.

80

Lesson 32

To the Teacher

Explain what is meant by a person's character. It is what he truly is on the inside, where it counts. Point out the strength of character that John Maynard possessed. He obeyed the captain's orders, thereby saving the lives of those on board even at the cost of his own life.

Be sure a map is available to help the students with exercise 7.

Describe how rosin and tar burn so the pupils understand why the fire could not be put out. In fact, water may only spread such a fire.

Discuss exercise 14 with the class. Point out that lack of physical description is not necessarily a weakness in a story, for it does not hinder our understanding. The plot in many stories is just as clear without the extra details. In this story the writer's purpose was to portray John Maynard's character, and he succeeded in doing so.

Compare this story with "A Simple Kind of Bravery." How were the story characters alike?

Discussion Starters

1. What is a helm? Why did John Maynard have to stay at the helm to save the people? (A helm is a wheel used to steer a ship. The ship had to be steered to the shore in order to save the people.)
2. Why did the captain want to keep the passengers from

9. Underline each word below that describes John Maynard.

selfish   <u>brave</u>   <u>honest</u>   <u>Christlike</u>   <u>intelligent</u>
weak-willed   rash   <u>skillful</u>   foolish   <u>respectful</u>

10. Why were the passengers told to go forward? Circle the letter of the best answer.

  a. They would have to jump off the front of the ship to be saved.
  b. Later they would have to go through fire to get to the front of the ship.
  c. The front of the ship would touch land first.
  (d.) For all the reasons above.

11. Why did the captain want to keep the passengers from abandoning the ship? Circle the letter of the best answer.

  (a.) The ship was too far from land.
  b. The captain thought the fire could be extinguished.
  c. The water was too cold.
  d. For all the reasons above.

12. What did John Maynard sacrifice to save the people on the ship? _his life_

13. Whose life was sacrificed to save the whole world? _Jesus' life_

C. Writing for Comprehension

14. For the purpose of this story, it is not necessary for us to know what John Maynard looked like. But as you were reading, you probably "saw" (visualized) John Maynard standing firmly at the helm and "heard" his steady voice. This shows us his character. On other paper, write a paragraph to describe the kind of man you think John Maynard was. Your description may use the words you underlined in exercise 9 above.
(Grade for originality and exactness of details.)

D. Review

15. Near the end of the story is a simile that tells how John Maynard stood at the helm. Write that simile.
firm as a rock

16. Write what is meant by visualizing. _seeing in our minds the events or scenes in a story_

leaving the ship even though it was burning? (There was a chance that the ship could reach shore. The passengers could have drowned if they had jumped overboard.)
3. What tells us that John Maynard was dying before he beached the ship? (He gave a feeble response.)
4. What lessons can we learn from John Maynard? (loyalty, faithfulness under extreme test, sacrifice of oneself to help others)

Fifth Reader Workbook

 33. Perseverance

It is amazing what we can do if we patiently work one step at a time. This is the only way we will ever accomplish anything worthwhile. Then if we have done our best, we can be happy even when we cannot do all we would like to do.

A. Defining for Comprehension

Find a word from the poem for each definition. The number in parentheses tells you in which stanza to find it.

1. Worthiest; loftiest; grandest. (4) __noblest__

2. Tasks; projects; jobs. (4) __undertakings__

3. Thought of; imagined. (4) __conceived__

4. Attained; accomplished. (4) __achieved__

5. Discouraged; depressed. (5) __disheartened__

6. Try; make an effort. (6) __endeavor__

7. Wise saying. (7) __proverb__

8. Keep on in spite of difficulties. (8) __persevere__

Circle the letter of the sentence that uses the underlined word in the same way as in the poem.

9. a. Father will <u>rent</u> a car to travel from the airport to the meeting.
   b. When Jesus died, the veil of the temple was <u>rent</u> in twain.
   c.) Jesus said that using new cloth to mend an old garment will make the <u>rent</u> worse.

10. a.) We should <u>resolve</u> to be kind.
    b. His <u>resolve</u> was to get the job done.

B. Reading for Comprehension

11. From the first two stanzas, list four small things that can make or do large things if repeated or laid one after another. __step, stitch, brick, flake__

12. Circle the letter of the sentence that best gives the thought of the fourth stanza.
    a. Only in doing the noblest things is it needful to be patient and to persevere.
    b. Some very great things have been accomplished one patient step at a time.
    c. As long as we persevere, we can do anything we set out to do.

13. Many things in nature grow very slowly, such as the oak tree from a tiny acorn. Which stanza of the poem refers to that fact? __stanza 7__

82

Lesson 33

To the Teacher

You may want to have the pupils read this poem chorally. Remind them to read at an even rate of speed, blending their voices together.

Ask the pupils what rhyme pattern the poem has. It should be easy for them to see that the second and fourth lines rhyme.

Discuss what is meant by *perseverance*. It is keeping on, little by little, until the task is done. When we look at a large task, it might appear almost impossible to do. Yet if we begin and then keep working a little at a time, we will be surprised at how soon the task is completed.

Nearly everything that is worthwhile requires perseverance. Schoolwork requires perseverance just as home duties do. A large building is not built in a day, and even a journey of a thousand miles begins with a single step.

Tell the pupils about coral. See Discussion Starters, number 3.

Discussion Starters

1. Name some jobs your parents do that take perseverance. (father in providing for the family; mother in daily tasks such as cooking, cleaning, and sewing; both parents in training children)
2. Do you think they could do these jobs if they had never learned to persevere? (no)

14. Circle the letter of the sentence that best gives the thought of the last stanza.

a. Determine to persevere in the duties you have now, rather than dreaming of doing great things beyond your ability.

b. Do not begin a worthwhile project unless you intend to complete it.

c. Never think of working at a distant place, but rather busy yourself at home.

15. Which virtue is most closely related to perseverance? Circle the letter of the best answer.

a. kindness   b. humility   c. patience

C. Writing for Comprehension

16. In what ways does God, through the trees and flowers of nature, teach us the lesson of patience and perseverance? Think of the tiny acorn growing to be a towering oak tree.

   (Sample answer.) Trees and flowers start from small seeds and grow very slowly. They are not "discouraged" even though it takes many years for some plants— especially trees—to grow. (An observant child may recognize that things done slowly and patiently are usually done right.)

17. a. Name four jobs that take perseverence.   (Sample answers.)
    washing dishes, hoeing a garden, writing a story, training a dog

    b. Now write a short paragraph about a time when you persevered or failed to persevere, and what the results were.

    (Individual paragraphs.)

D. Review

18. Notice the rhyme pattern of this poem. Which two lines in each stanza rhyme?

    lines 2 and 4

Write whether each sentence is true (T) or false (F).

T 19. A wary animal would be watchful.

F 20. A succulent plant would be dried up.

T 21. **Aye** is pronounced as a long **i** (ī) when it means "yes."

83

3. What is coral? How does it make islands? (Coral is a hard formation made of the skeletons of tiny sea animals. Millions of these animals live together; and as they die, their skeletons slowly build up until they form a coral island.)

4. What will happen if we daydream? (We will waste time that we should be using to do worthwhile things.)

Fifth Reader Workbook

34. Mary's Bible

The girl in this story greatly longed to have a Bible. Because the Bible is so readily available to us, we might not value it as we should. Let us esteem the Bible as a priceless treasure indeed, for it shows the way to God and eternal life.

A. Defining for Comprehension

Part I

Write the correct words in the blanks after the sentences below. You will not use all the words.

account	wayside	utterly	prey
provisions	smite	enterprise	hamlet
turf	vast	poised	benighted

1. John gave an interesting ___ of his trip to Mexico. _____account_____

2. Anna's mother gave her food and other ___ for the journey. _____provisions_____

3. God said that He would ___ the people of Egypt with great plagues. _smite_____

4. To be completely defeated is to be ___ defeated. _____utterly_____

5. One traveler fell by the ___ and could go no farther. _____wayside_____

6. The eagle sat ___ on the branch, ready to fly into the air. _____poised_____

7. The ___ prairie stretched for miles into the distance. _____vast_____

8. If rabbits are careless, they soon become the ___ of hawks. _____prey_____

9. To be ___ in the forest can be a frightening experience. _____benighted_____

10. A ___ is a small village. _____hamlet_____

Part II

Match the following words with their definitions.

_e_ 11. petition   a. Surround; enclose.

_g_ 12. gravely   b. Genuine; sincere.

_b_ 13. unaffected   c. Spoke uncertainly; stammered.

_h_ 14. moor   d. Completely overcoming.

_f_ 15. consistent   e. Request; appeal.

_c_ 16. faltered   f. Faithful; doing what one says.

_a_ 17. envelop   g. Seriously; solemnly.

_d_ 18. overwhelming   h. Stretch of wasteland.

84

Lesson 34

To the Teacher

Explain to the students that Bibles were very scarce in the area where Mary Jones lived. Use a map to show where Wales is.

Point out the great love that Mary had for the Word of God, and ask the students to find two facts in the story that are proof of this. (She had worked and saved for six years to earn enough money for a Bible. She walked twenty-five miles to buy one.) Help them to grasp the great distance Mary walked by naming a point about twenty-five miles (40 km) from your school.

Point out the far-reaching effect of Mary's effort. It is thought that the incident helped to increase the printing of Bibles in the Welsh language. As a result, many more of Mary's fellow citizens were able to have the Word of God in their own homes.

Link this story to the previous poem, "Perseverance." Day by day Mary worked toward her goal of owning a Bible until finally she reached it.

Discuss exercise 34 in class. Help students to gain a proper understanding of a summary. Some may tend to include too many details, while others may skip main points for the sake of brevity.

This lesson is longer than usual and may be divided. If you do this, assign exercises 1–10 and 27–30 with Part I of the story, and exercises 11–26 and 31–36 with Part II. (In Discussion Starters, numbers 1–4 are for Part I and numbers 5–9 are for Part II.)

m	19. clasped	i. Respectful; worshipful.
p	20. blustering	j. The heavens; sky.
l	21. unconscious	k. Great; vast.
o	22. looms	l. Not aware.
n	23. radiance	m. Held tightly; grasped.
i	24. reverent	n. Brightness; glow.
k	25. extensive	o. Machines that weave cloth.
j	26. firmament	p. Blowing gustily.

B. Reading for Comprehension

27. Write the sentence near the beginning of the story which tells us that Mary was a persevering young woman who loved the Word of God.

     After working and saving for six years, this was the day she was going for her Bible!

28. Before Mary left, what important thing did the family do for her protection? _____

     They prayed together.

29. One sentence says that Mary passed through an area where there was "little sign of habitation." In the list below, underline the names of things that you would **not** expect to see in such a place.

     <u>buildings</u>   trees   <u>cows in a meadow</u>   <u>wheat fields</u>
     rocks   <u>vehicles</u>   a waterfall   <u>fences</u>

30. At one point in the story, Mary seemed almost ready to give up and return home. Write the sentence that gives this idea.

     She stood poised, unable to move, a prey for the first time to doubt. (or) Suddenly her enterprise loomed up before her as something beyond her strength, and she felt the clutch of panic at her heart.

31. Why could Mr. Charles not quickly get more Bibles?

     The Society (Bible Society) had refused to print more Bibles for Wales.

32. At one point in the story, Mr. Charles said, "And this is only one illustration of the terrible need for Bibles in Wales." What illustration was he talking about?

     No Bible was available for Mary after she had saved for years and walked many miles to get one.

Literary concept in this lesson:

Summary (See exercise 34.)

Discussion Starters

1. Name several things which show that Mary was very brave. (She set out by herself on a 25-mile walk. She walked through places where hardly anyone lived. She had to cross the shoulder of a mountain. She kept going even when weariness and doubt troubled her.)

2. What did Mary do to help keep up her courage? (She repeated verses from Psalm 121, including "I will lift up mine eyes unto the hills, from whence cometh my help" and "The LORD shall preserve thee from all evil: he shall preserve thy soul.")

3. Why did Mary say, "I work very hard too," in a quiet voice? (The farm girl seemed to think that Mary had time to go on walks for pleasure.)

4. What are the people of Wales called? What are they always glad to do? (The people are called Welsh. They are always ready to direct a stranger, even if it means going out of their way to do so.)

5. Why was Mary trembling just before breakfast? (She was about to go to the Bible seller's house, and she trembled with nervousness at the thought.)

6. What did Mr. Charles think at first that Mary would want? (He expected to hear a petition for work or other help of some kind.)

Fifth Reader Workbook

C. Writing for Comprehension

33. Why did Mr. Charles give Mary a Bible even though he did not have one to spare? _____
    He saw how heartbroken she was at the thought of not getting a Bible.

34. A *summary* is a paragraph that sums up the most important details of a story. It tells in just a few sentences what a story is about. A summary should include the most important characters, the setting, the main idea, and the main events.

    Write a summary of "Mary's Bible" on other paper. It should have six or seven sentences in all. You may begin with the boldface sentence below.

    "Mary's Bible" is a story about a persevering young girl who lived in Wales in 1802.
    (See sample summary below.)

D. Review

35. Read again the paragraph in Part II that begins, "As Mr. Charles spoke." Three sentences in this paragraph contain figures of speech. Write these three figures.

    a. __(fell) like stones on Mary's ears_____

    b. __(envelop her) like a cloud_____

    c. __(rise up) like a great wave_____

36. Because all these figures of speech begin with **like,** they are all (similes, metaphors).

Sample summary for Part C

"Mary's Bible" is a story about a persevering young girl who lived in Wales in 1802. She loved the Word of God so much that she worked and saved for six years to buy her own Bible. Mary had to walk twenty-five miles to reach the home of Mr. Charles, who sold Bibles. But when she got there, Mr. Charles told Mary that he had not one Bible that she could have. But when he saw Mary's great sorrow at this news, Mr. Charles let her have a Bible after all. The story ends with a radiant Mary arriving home to share her treasure, the Book of books, with her joyous parents.

86

---

7. Name several things that showed Mary's deep interest in the Bible. (She learned to read it. She walked two miles every Saturday to study it. She memorized many Scriptures. She knew most of Jesus' parables and the Sermon on the Mount.)

8. Why did Mary cry so much? (Mr. Charles said that he had no Bible for her, which meant that Mary's hard work and long walk were all for nothing.)

9. Describe the differences between Mary's walk to Bala and her walk home. (On the walk to Bala, Mary grew tired, hungry, and thirsty. On the walk home, Mary was so happy that weariness, hunger, and thirst went unnoticed.)

35. The Oil or the Book

We should be thankful that we can read, for it is an important aid in serving God. Being able to read the Bible is an especially great privilege. The people in this story became a "new" family because they learned to read the best Book.

A. Defining for Comprehension

Match these words from the story with their definitions. You will not use all the definitions.

__c__	1. lowlanders	a.	Monotonous or repetitious speech or song.
__e__	2. coarsely	b.	Speaking or humming in low, dull tones.
__h__	3. tropical	c.	People who live in valleys or plains.
__b__	4. droning	d.	Heathen; idolatrous.
__d__	5. pagan (pā′ gən)	e.	Roughly; crudely.
__a__	6. chant	f.	Following a winding course.
__g__	7. primers (prĭm′ ərz)	g.	Simple books used to teach reading.
		h.	Having to do with warm regions of the earth.

Use six of the words listed above to fill the blanks in the sentences below.

8. Some __lowlanders__ who live in __tropical__ regions build their houses on stilts because of the wet climate.

9. A number of __pagan__ worshipers, dressed in __coarsely__ woven clothes, were __droning__ a strange __chant__ to their idol.

B. Reading for Comprehension

10. Find a map of the Philippines in an encyclopedia or other reference book. Then underline the correct word in the following sentence.
Mindanao is the (northernmost, southernmost, easternmost, westernmost) of the main islands in the Philippines.

11. What Book does the title refer to? __the Bible__

Lesson 35

To the Teacher

Find the Philippine Islands on a map, and point out the island of Mindanao. You might also draw a sketch of Zaidan's bark house on poles. Explain that the houses on the islands are built on poles because of the heavy rainfall, which brings the danger of flooding.

Point out the privilege it is to be able to read. Tell the students to imagine going to church and not being able to hold the hymnal right-side up, or to turn to the passage that the minister is reading. Truly we are blessed.

Discuss the truth in what Zaidan's mother said about worshiping idols and not even needing to think. Every person has a desire to worship something. Zaidan's father had chosen the easy way in his attempt to satisfy that inner hunger.

Note that the first three and the last three paragraphs of the story are similar except for the fact that Father goes with them at the end. He is no longer ashamed, because now he can read.

Be sure to discuss Part C before assigning it. You might want to make a list of points.

Literary concept in this lesson:

Reading for details (Discuss exercise 17 in class.)

Fifth Reader Workbook

In exercises 12–14, circle the letter of the best answer.

12. The story says that the huts in Zaidan's village were made of bark. Why do you think the people used that material?

   a. They lived in a wet climate.

   b. It took very little effort to build houses of bark.

   c. Bark was inexpensive and plentiful.

   d. For all the reasons above.

13. Why did Zaidan's father find it easier to worship the oil than to serve the true God?

   a. He did not have to learn anything new.

   b. He did not have to think.

   c. He did not need to feel ashamed of being unable to read.

   d. For all the reasons above.

14. Why do you think Zaidan's father had never learned to read before?

   a. He was too lazy.

   b. He had no interest in reading.

   c. He had never had a good opportunity to learn to read.

   d. For all the reasons above.

15. What made it difficult for Zaidan to keep up with her class in school? _____

   ___She could not always attend school._____

16. The first three paragraphs of the story are similar to the last three paragraphs. What one thing in particular makes them different?

   ___Zaidan's father was with his family in the last three paragraphs._____

   _____

17. To **read for details** is to read with close attention in order to find facts. Read the first paragraph of "The Oil or the Book." Then write at least five details to make a list of facts about the main character and her surroundings. One detail is given as an example.

   The main character is a girl named Zaidan.   (Sample details listed.)

   _Zaidan is of the Bagobo tribe._____   She lives in a bark hut.

   _The house has a ladder going up to it.__   The house is in the hills near Mindanao.

   _Mindanao is one of the Philippine Islands.__

   Zaidan has had a bath in a cold stream.   Zaidan has light brown skin.

   _The lowlanders lived on the plains.____   The stream flowed from the hills to the plain.

88

Discussion Starters

1. Why did Zaidan and her family hardly notice the beauty of the tropical scenery? (They saw it so often that it was common to them.)

2. Why was Zaidan so eager to learn to read? (She wanted to teach her parents how to read.)

3. When Zaidan's father was ashamed to go to church, why did he not simply stay away from any kind of worship? (He felt that he must worship something, so he returned to pagan worship.)

4. What are some things you think happened in that little Bagobo barrio that summer? (The young man taught reading classes. Zaidan's parents and many other people learned to read. Zaidan's father stopped worshiping the oil and started going to church again.)

5. Why is the title a good one for this story? (In the story, Zaidan's father had to decide whether to worship the oil or to live by the Bible.)

6. Why was the visiting man called a lowlander? What does this tell about where Zaidan's family probably lived? (The visiting man was called a lowlander because he lived in a lowland region. So Zaidan's family probably lived in the highlands—the hills or mountains.)

C. Writing for Comprehension

18. Being unable to read was a great hindrance to Zaidan's father. But notice that her mother was faithful to God even though she could not read. Being unable to read is no excuse for turning away from God, but reading is surely a blessing that helps us better serve God.

   Write a paragraph explaining why being able to read is a blessing. Be sure to include the most important reason, which has already been mentioned.

   (Sample points to be included; the most important is first.)
   We can learn for ourselves what God says, rather than depending on others to tell us. (They might not always be truthful.) We can learn about people, places, and events that we would never know about otherwise. We can receive encouragement and blessing from letters that our friends send us. We can save ourselves trouble and pain by reading signs that warn us of danger.

Fifth Reader Workbook

 # 36. The Rich Fool

One truth we should learn from this story is that the rich man did not have a generous heart. This is evident in his decision to store all his goods in bigger barns and keep them for himself. He said, "There will I bestow all my fruits and my goods." He did not consider sharing his goods. Neither did he seem to realize that God had given them to him, and that he was therefore responsible to God for how he used them.

The account of the rich fool is a ***parable.*** A simple definition of a parable is "an earthly story with a heavenly meaning." Jesus used parables to teach truth to those who listened to Him, much as your teacher uses examples and illustrations to explain things to you.

For this composition assignment, write a poem about sharing your blessings with others. Write two stanzas with four lines each (or whatever your teacher tells you). You may want to use the same rhyme and rhythm patterns found in the poem "Growing Smiles" in Lesson 21. Regardless of what rhyme and rhythm patterns you use, be consistent. Make sure all your lines match the pattern you begin with. You may choose a title from below or make up one of your own if you prefer.

Our Duty to Share
Not Mine, but God's
Remember the Needs of Others
A Heart That Loves

Title: _____

(Teacher: You may want to help students get started by working on a few lines together, but try to inspire them to be original and creative. You may want to assign only one stanza to slower students.)

90

Lesson 36

To the Teacher

Read this parable aloud to the students, and discuss its meaning. Help them to see the danger in the rich man's attitude. He was concerned only about the natural things and not about spiritual things. Though outwardly he was rich, he was a beggar inwardly.

How does the poem "Our Daily Bread" relate to this parable? The poem points out that God is the supreme Giver, a fact that the rich man failed to recognize. Had he considered it, he would have thought about God when he asked, "What shall I do?" He would have distributed his goods to the poor instead of hoarding them for himself.

Pay special heed to the opening verse of the parable, which sums up the truth very well: "A man's life consisteth not in the abundance of the things which he possesseth." Also consider the last verse. *So* means "just like this rich man"— and that includes the fact that God said he was a fool.

Tell the students to work on their poems on other paper first. Encourage them to rewrite their poems until their work is the best they can do and then write the poems neatly in the workbooks. Grade for neatness as well as content.

Literary concept in this lesson:

Parable

Review for Test 6

1. Be sure you know the meanings of the vocabulary words in Lessons 31–36.

2. Be sure you know what these terms mean. The last three are from earlier lessons.

   summary (Lesson 34)
   reading for details (Lesson 35)
   parable (Lesson 36)
   figures of speech (Lesson 7)
   visualizing (Lesson 19)
   verifying (Lesson 22)

Discussion Starters

1. What is covetousness? (greed; the desire for more and more things)

2. How could we be like the rich fool? (We could become so involved with getting things and taking care of them that we forget about serving God and helping others.)

3. What should we do with the blessings God gives us? (Use them for the glory of God. Share generously with others.)

4. What blessings do we receive from sharing? (Sharing brings joy. It is a way of laying up treasure in heaven. Often God blesses the giver in natural ways too.)

5. Can we take riches to heaven? (No; but by giving money to needy people and to the Lord's work, we lay up treasure in heaven.)

6. Are the things we have really ours? (No; everything belongs to God.)

Fifth Reader Workbook

 37. Rebellion in the Hive

This story could be called a fable because it pictures bees acting like people. Its purpose is to teach a lesson about submission and cooperation. When we are tempted to rebel, let us remember that taking our own way will rob us of the very happiness we are trying to find.

A. Defining for Comprehension

Match these words from the story with their definitions.

c	1. distinguish	a.	Imagine; visualize.
g	2. composure	b.	Shoemaker.
f	3. drones	c.	Tell apart; know the difference.
b	4. cobbler	d.	Watchmen; guards.
a	5. fancy	e.	Spread out; scattered.
i	6. ambitious	f.	Male bees.
j	7. wretched	g.	Calmness; presence of mind.
e	8. dispersed	h.	Usual; familiar.
h	9. accustomed	i.	Eager to do or have something.
d	10. sentinels	j.	Miserable; unhappy; distressed.

B. Reading for Comprehension

11. Compare the beginning of Part I with the beginning of Part II, noticing the difference in the moods. A *mood* is the general feeling of a person or group. Part I has a bright, joyous mood, whereas Part II has a dark, unhappy mood.

    List five words from the first paragraph of Part I, and five words from the first two paragraphs of Part II, which help to produce those moods.

    (Any five in each column)

Bright Mood (Part I)	**Dark Mood (Part II)**
lovely, brightly, warm,	dark, heavy, cloud,
bright, colorful, delight, treasure	discontented, rebelled,
(In older editions: beautiful, gay)	angrily, wretched

92

Lesson 37

To the Teacher

This story brings out the folly of rebellion, and the disorder that results when there is no teamwork. Help students to see the need of leaders in the home, the school, and the church.

What was wrong with Uncle Collins's reasoning? He failed to realize that some people are gifted in the area of leadership, whereas others fit in better as workers. It is not that one is more important than the other, because they are all needed. The king would be in a sad condition without a cobbler to make his shoes, and the cobbler needs the king to rule over him and give him protection.

Point out the interesting fact that the bee was perfectly contented with her station in life until someone came along and told her how "wretched" she was. Our attitude toward ourselves and our work can make all the difference between happiness and misery.

Emphasize the wisdom and stability shown by the older bee. Although she was weaker physically, her experience had brought with it wisdom beyond that of the traveler bee.

You may wish to close the discussion with Scriptures that command us to be subject to those in authority over us. God established this for our good so that we can lead happy, well-ordered lives.

Note: In older editions of the reader, the traveler bee and other workers are referred to as "he," "him," and "fellows."

12. Uncle Collins said, "Nature never makes one man a king and another a cobbler." According to Daniel 2:20, 21, who sets up kings? ___God___

13. Uncle Collins wrongly influenced the children who found the traveler bee. Circle the letter of two statements below which show that Uncle Collins did not respect the order that God established among men.

   ⓐ "He said that kings and queens are not right."
   ⓑ "Uncle Collins says all people who work for other people and don't work for themselves are poor wretches."
   c. "He said that the worker bees are just the same as the queen when they are first born."
   d. "Fancy how angry these workers would be if they knew what else the gardener told me!"

14. Fill in the blanks with words from Proverbs 12:15.

   The traveler bee acted like a foolish person when he thought his own way was _____right_____. The traveler bee acted like a wise person when he listened to the _____counsel_____ of the old relation.

15. In Part II, find the paragraph that says the traveler bee was "ashamed and unhappy." Then circle the letters of three sentences below that give reasons for the bee's distress.

   ⓐ She was ashamed of the way she and others had acted.
   b. She was angry with the old relation.
   ⓒ She was unhappy with the way things were turning out.
   d. She did not like to work alone.
   ⓔ She was failing to do her job of gathering honey and pollen.
   f. She was upset because the others would not let her be the queen.

16. What is the main idea of this story? Circle the letter of the best answer.

   a. All men are created alike and equal.
   b. No one is wretched until he is told that he is.
   ⓒ Someone must be the leader if a group is to live and work together well.

This is not accurate, for worker bees are actually undeveloped females. However, the workbook exercises are still compatible with older editions except that number 15 uses *she* instead of *he*. You may want to explain this if students are using an older edition.

Literary concept in this lesson:

Mood words (Discuss exercise 11 in class.)

Discussion Starters

1. What was wrong with Uncle Collins's ideas? (They were the ideas of someone who was discontented and rebellious. The Bible says that such attitudes are wrong and teaches that we should be content and submissive.)

2. What does God want children to do in relation to their parents and teachers? (Obey them.)

3. Does God consider servants less important than kings? (No; all people are equally important to God.)

4. Why did the bees find it impossible to work together after they left the hive? (Nobody wanted to give up to anyone else.)

5. What shows you that the old relation was very wise? (She knew that if even two people live together, one must be the leader and one the follower. If there is a multitude, how much more must there be appointed leaders and followers.)

6. At what point in the story did the young worker recognize her mistake? (She recognized it when she said, "Don't laugh at me. Tell me what to do.")

Fifth Reader Workbook

C. Writing for Comprehension

17. At one point the traveler bee said, "Don't laugh at me. Tell me what to do." In your own words, write what the old relation told the traveler bee to make his song happy once again.

    (Sample answer.) The old relation told the traveler bee that different bees are
    suited for different kinds of work. For any group to live together peaceably, one
    must be the head and the others must contentedly fill their places.
    _____
    _____

18. Animals cannot talk, of course, but we can learn lessons from them.

    a. What lesson can we learn from this story? _(Sample answers.) being content with_
       where God puts us, submitting to those in authority, cooperating with others

    b. Tell about another animal that we can learn a lesson from. _(Sample answer.)_
       The ant teaches us to work so that we have food for winter.

94

38. The Brickfields of Bristol

At the time of George Whitefield and John Wesley, people in England were sharply divided between the rich and the poor. Because churches were mostly for the wealthy, common people of the day had little opportunity to hear the Gospel. Whitefield and Wesley had compassion on the poor and began to preach in outdoor meetings. Instead of despising the needy, they did what they could to help them.

A. Defining for Comprehension

These words are found in the story. Write the correct ones in the blanks after sentences 1–8.

tawdry	entreating
denounced	similar
outskirts	occasion
sullen	astonishment

1. The Smiths moved from a house downtown to the ___ of the city.   outskirts

2. The unhappy child had a ___ look on his face.   sullen

3. The ___ dress looked out of place among the fine clothes.   tawdry

4. Uncle Harry had an experience ___ to yours.   similar

5. Various prophets ___ the evil deeds of the people.   denounced

6. The parents were ___ their children to behave wisely.   entreating

7. The meeting gave Father an ___ to speak about the Lord.   occasion

8. To Mother's ___, the dish that fell was not broken.   astonishment

9. Tell what is meant by "open-air preaching" and "outdoor evangelism." _____
   preaching out in fields rather than in church buildings

B. Reading for Comprehension

10. At the beginning of the story, the stall owner looked at Wesley and said, "He's ridden a long way!" How could he tell this? _____
    The horse stumbled, and the rider almost slipped from the saddle.

11. Why do you think John Wesley was banned from the church pulpits in London for his fiery, Bible-centered messages? Circle the letter of the best answer.
    a. He was not rich.
    b. He did not have a pleasant voice.
    c. The people did not like to hear the truth.

Lesson 38

To the Teacher

Give some background information about John Wesley, the noted English evangelist. Mention that he was a brother of Charles Wesley, who wrote over 6,500 hymns.

Contrast the ministry of Whitefield and Wesley with that of the common English preachers of that time. How were they different? (Whitefield and Wesley were concerned about helping the poorer English people, whereas most of the other preachers lived mainly for themselves.) The conversation at the beginning of the story portrays this well. Explain that most common people did not attend services because the preachers had little interest in their spiritual welfare.

Discuss the pillory and the whipping post, which were both common means of punishment in England during the early 1700s.

It would also be good to compare John Wesley's preaching with Christ's. In what three ways were they alike? (They both preached to the poor, both preached to large crowds of people, and both were despised by the religious leaders of the day.)

Point out the skillful way the author changes viewpoints between the fourth and fifth paragraphs of the story. First we see Wesley as others saw him, a tired preacher; then we see him as he was on the inside, looking out.

Literary concept in this lesson:

Biography (Discuss exercise 14 in class.)

Fifth Reader Workbook

12. The story suggests that the poor, working people stayed away from worship services because they did not fit into the high-class churches of the day. According to their response to the work of Whitefield and Wesley, these people did want to hear the Gospel. Copy a sentence from Mark 12:37 which says that the ordinary people also responded readily to Jesus' words.

    "And the common people heard him gladly."

13. What did John and George probably talk about when they walked home from the meeting at Rose Green?

    George asked John to take over his work and to preach at Nicholas Street that evening.

14. Today's story is taken from the book *Horseman of the King,* by Cyril Davey. That book is a **biography** of John Wesley.

    a. What is a biography?   a written account of a person's life

    b. Give the title and author of one other biography that you know of.

       (Individual work. You may have to verify answers.)

15. Find a hymn written by Charles Wesley, the brother of John Wesley. Give its title, the name of the songbook where you found it, and the number of the song.

    (Sample answer: "Love Divine, All Love Excelling"—*Christian Hymnal,* number 43, or *Church Hymnal,* number 84)

C. Writing for Comprehension

16. From the information given in the story, explain how Whitefield and Wesley were different from most preachers in England at that time.   (Sample answers.)

    Most preachers lived in luxury, but Whitefield and Wesley lived simple lives. Most preachers cared little about poor people, but Whitefield and Wesley had compassion on the poor.

17. In your own words, describe the houses and the children of the poor people that John Wesley saw at Kingswood.

    (Descriptions should give the following details in the pupils' own words.)
    The houses were "square brick boxes, dirty outside and probably filthy inside."
    The children were "thin, ill kempt, and dressed in rags."

96

Note: Although Wesley, Whitefield, and their contemporaries did many good things, there were deficiencies in their work. None of them insisted on a life of separation from the world, and many "conversions" in their revival movement were mere emotional experiences that failed to produce holy living.

Discussion Starters

1. According to the stall owner and the woman, how did most preachers view country folk? (Most preachers did not think much about helping country folk.)
2. Why did they feel this way? (Preachers' main interests seemed to be fox hunting and eating and drinking with their rich neighbors.)
3. Why were the common people so eager to hear the Gospel? (They were not welcome in the churches of that time. The Gospel was a message of hope and love.)
4. What is slag? What were the brickfields? (Slag is the material left over after metal is removed from ore. Brickfields were brickyards, the areas around the kilns where bricks were made.)
5. Whenever George Whitefield spoke of someone to take his place, "John avoided his glance." Why did he do this? (He was not sure about being the one to fill that place.)
6. What moved the people to tears when John Wesley preached? (He told them about the love of God.)
7. Had John Wesley cared about the poor earlier in his life? (Yes; the poor people of Bristol reminded him of the ones in London, whom he had wanted to talk to.)

D. Review

*Write whether each sentence is true (**T**) or false (**F**).*

   T   18. A wretched person is an unhappy person.

   T   19. Male bees are called drones.

   F   20. To fancy something means to doubt it.

   T   21.   A biography is the story of a person's life.

Fifth Reader Workbook

 39. God Is Love

The poem tells us that God is both light and love. Love is like light in that it can drive hatred out of the heart just as light can drive darkness out of a room. God's love is like a light that guides us through a dark world and gives us comfort and cheer.

A. Defining for Comprehension

1. Use the following words in sentences of your own.
   a. bliss ___great happiness; joy___ (Words should have the meanings given.)
   b. woe ___deep distress or misery___
   c. decay ___rot; break down___
   d. comfort ___reassurance; consolation___

2. This poem uses some words with the **-eth** ending, such as in **waneth** and **entwineth.** This is an old way of saying **wanes** and **entwines.** Write a definition for each word.
   a. wane ___diminish; become weaker___
   b. entwine ___twist together; mix in___

B. Reading for Comprehension

3. For each statement, write the line from the poem that has the same meaning.
   a. God gives great happiness and eases suffering.
      ___Bliss He forms, and woe He lightens.___
   b. Nations break down, and time goes on.
      ___Worlds decay, and ages move.___
   c. God's mercy never becomes weaker.
      ___But His mercy waneth never.___
   d. Even when life seems to have no light at all
      ___E'en the hour that darkest seemeth.___

4. The third stanza says that even in the darkest hour, God's brightness streams from the mist. Try to visualize this word picture. Then circle the letter of the phrase that best describes the picture.
   a. A neon sign flashing outside your window at night.
   b. A red light flashing at a dark intersection.
   c. A lighthouse shining its beam into foggy darkness.
   d. A flashlight shining into a dark room.

98

Lesson 39

To the Teacher

Discuss the message of this poem, being sure the students understand the meanings of the more difficult words.

Ask the students what the rhyme pattern is. (The first and third lines rhyme, as do the second and fourth lines.) Then ask them to describe the rhythm pattern. (It begins with an accented syllable, and alternates between accented and unaccented syllables.) Compare this pattern with the pattern in the poem "Growing Smiles."

Discuss Bible verses, especially from 1 John, which tell us that God is light and love. Light is the opposite of darkness; yet it is not the direct opposite, for light is stronger than darkness.

When light enters a place, darkness flees; but there is no such thing as directing darkness into a room and chasing out the light. Use this illustration to draw a parallel between hatred and love.

This poem is a hymn found in many hymnbooks. Sing it with your students if practical.

You may want to do exercises 8 and 9 with the students.

Literary concept in this lesson:

Rhythm patterns (Discuss exercise 6 in class.)

5. The last line of each stanza is the same. The first part of the lines comes from 1 John 1 and the second part from 1 John 4. Write the complete reference for each part.

   a. God is light. <u>1 John 1:5</u>

   b. God is love. <u>1 John 4:8 or 16</u>

6. This poem has been set to music and is a familiar hymn to many people. Before a poem can be set to music, it must have a consistent ***rhythm pattern.*** Below is the first stanza of "God Is Love." Write / above each accented syllable and ∪ above each unaccented syllable to show its accent pattern.

   / ∪ / ∪ / ∪ / ∪
   God is love, His mer-cy bright-ens
   / ∪ / ∪ / ∪ /
   All the path in which we move;
   / ∪ / ∪ / ∪ / ∪
   Bliss He forms, and woe He light-ens;
   / ∪ / ∪ / ∪ /
   God is light, and God is love.

7. This poem also has a consistent rhyme pattern. Copy the rhyming words in the first stanza as described below.

   a. a pair of words that rhyme exactly <u>brightens, lightens</u>

   b. a pair of words that nearly rhyme <u>move, love</u>

C. Writing for Comprehension

8. Summarize the thought of the first three lines in the second stanza.

   <u>Worldly things are constantly changing and decaying as time moves on, but God's</u>
   <u>mercy never becomes less.</u>

9. Summarize the thought of the first two lines in the last stanza.

   <u>God mixes hope and comfort from heaven with our earthly cares.</u>

Discussion Starters

1. What are some things that God's light can shine away or shine through? (the darkness of fear, by bringing love; the darkness of doubt, by bringing faith; the darkness of ignorance, by bringing the knowledge of God)

2. What are some things in this world that are always changing? (The earth's surface changes through earthquakes, floods, and volcanoes. The weather is always changing. People become older. New buildings are put up and old ones torn down. Nations rise and fall; rulers come and go.)

3. Give the word that means
   a. time. (hour)
   b. nations. (worlds)
   c. fog or cloud. (mist)
   d. troubles or concerns. (cares)

Fifth Reader Workbook

D. Review

*Write whether each sentence is true (**T**) or false (**F**).*

___T___ 10. A biography is the story of a person's life.

___T___ 11. Any composition that is not a poem is considered prose.

___F___ 12. All poetry must have rhyming words.

___T___ 13. One benefit of research is to better understand what we read.

40. The Lost Boy

When a person selfishly takes his own way, it is often at someone else's expense. The boy in this story did not stop to think of the grief he might cause others as well as himself by his disobedience.

A. Defining for Comprehension

Try to match the following words to their meanings by using the context. Use a dictionary only if necessary.

<u>b</u>   1. remote   a. Came forth in a stream.

<u>d</u>   2. venture   b. Far away from settled areas; distant.

<u>h</u>   3. borne   c. Thin, as from starvation; gaunt.

<u>a</u>   4. issued   d. Dare to go.

<u>f</u>   5. unabated   e. Tiredness; weariness.

<u>g</u>   6. mustered   f. Undiminished; not slackened.

<u>c</u>   7. emaciated   g. Called or gathered together; assembled.

<u>e</u>   8. fatigue   h. Carried; swept.

Study the meaning of each word, and use it in a sentence of your own. **(Individual sentences.)**

9. vigor—energetic zeal; active strength. _____

_____

10. revived—made active; stirred up again. _____

_____

11. hazard—risk; danger. _____

_____

B. Reading for Comprehension

How well did you concentrate? Without looking back at the story, circle the letters of the correct answers in numbers 12–16. If you must look back for an answer, write **X** *beside the number of that question.*

12. What was Charles's last name?
   a. Mason
   b. Maser
   c. Mosser

Lesson 40

To the Teacher

Locate Maine on a wall map and point out the many coves along its coastline. Explain that these sheltered areas help to keep boats safe from the rough storms of the open sea.

Read Ephesians 6:1–4, paying special attention to verse 3. God gave us certain commandments to obey for our own well-being. Discuss how Charles would have been much better off if he had obeyed his father.

Again discuss how tides operate. Two times daily they come in and go out, due to the gravity of the moon.

Consider with the pupils how nearly Charles missed being seen. It was by God's providence that the author turned around for that final glance and saw Charles.

The last paragraph merits special attention. How important it is to always be obedient!

Discussion Starters

1. Why did nobody see Charles leaving in the boat? (He was playing by himself. Most of the fishermen were at sea.)
2. Why did Charles's boat go out to sea? (The tide went out.)
3. How would you describe Charles's personality? (He was thoughtless but brave. He kept up his courage even though he passed one island after another.)
4. How do you know that he was very familiar with his surroundings? (He was not frightened at first, for he

Fifth Reader Workbook

13. In what state did the story take place?
    a. New Hampshire
    (b.) Maine
    c. Connecticut

14. In what month did the story take place?
    a. March
    (b.) August
    c. December

15. What caused Charles's boat to move away from the shore?
    (a.) tide
    b. wind
    c. waves

16. About how far did Charles drift before he landed on the island?
    a. two miles
    b. six miles
    (c.) ten miles

17. Who was at fault because Charles drifted away in the little boat? Read Ephesians 6:1–3. Then circle the letter of the best answer, and explain why you chose that answer.
    a. Charles's parents   (b.) Charles himself   c. the owner of the boat
    Charles did not obey to his father, so it did not go well with him.

18. Why did Charles not answer his rescuers when he heard their shouts? _____
    He was too weak to answer.

19. What did Charles eat on the island?   wild berries

20. When Charles was found, how nearly was it that the men had missed seeing him? _____
    The men were leaving the island when one of them looked back and saw Charles.

21. Circle the letter of the sentence below that best tells what lesson this story teaches.
    a. It is very dangerous to play with boats unless our parents are near.
    (b.) One act of disobedience can bring great trouble to ourselves as well as others.
    c. If we do not willingly obey our parents, we may be taken away from them.

102

expected to be carried back in by the tide. Later he hoped to land on the last island, which was about ten miles out.)

5. Why were the author and the father the only ones who searched the far island? (Stormy weather made it dangerous for small boats to be out on the water.)

6. Why is disobedience harmful? (It causes trouble for ourselves and for those who love us.)

7. Who would be affected if you should be missing for several days? (The people affected would include your family, school, church, and relatives, and probably the police.)

C. Writing for Comprehension

22. Write a paragraph explaining how Charles's disobedience affected other people.

     (Paragraph should mention his parents' grief and the resulting physical condition

     of his mother. It should also mention the distress and inconvenience that the vil-

     lagers suffered because of it.)

23. Write three questions that Charles must have asked himself while he was on the island. ____

     (Sample answers.)

     Will anyone find me?   What will I eat?

     Where will I sleep?   Why did I disobey?

D. Review

24. Write whether each sentence is true (**T**) or false (**F**).

     __F__   a. The narrator of this story is Mr. Mason.

     __T__   b. The main character in this story is Charles.

     __F__   c. Rhythm is the use of words whose endings sound alike.

25. Give the title of another story that you have studied in this reader, in which people brought

     back someone who had drifted out to sea.   "The Rescue" (Lesson 25)

Fifth Reader Workbook

 41. The Beautiful Home

A beautiful house does not necessarily make a beautiful home. A beautiful home is a place where people have beautiful lives because they love each other. It is much more important to have a beautiful home than a beautiful house.

A. Defining for Comprehension

Match the following words to their definitions. You may use a dictionary.

_i_	1. picturesque	a.	Irremovably; permanently.
_c_	2. conveniences	b.	Lean and strong.
_a_	3. indelibly	c.	Modern appliances.
_h_	4. linoleum	d.	Hired; employed.
_j_	5. wistfully	e.	Close examination.
_f_	6. installed	f.	Put in place to be used.
_d_	7. engaged	g.	Neighboring; bordering.
_b_	8. wiry	h.	Floor covering.
_e_	9. scrutiny	i.	Beautiful; attractive.
_g_	10. adjoining	j.	Wishfully; longingly.

_n_	11. spacious	k.	Said mournfully.
_p_	12. exquisitely	l.	Poorness; neediness.
_s_	13. apologetically	m.	Make aware; inform.
_m_	14. acquaint	n.	Large and open; roomy.
_q_	15. reluctant	o.	Mood; general feeling.
_t_	16. deprived	p.	Elegantly; elaborately.
_r_	17. sympathetically	q.	Unwilling; opposed.
_k_	18. lamented	r.	With consideration; compassionately.
_o_	19. atmosphere	s.	Regretfully; remorsefully.
_l_	20. poverty	t.	Forced to do without; denied.

104

Lesson 41

To the Teacher

In reading this story orally, concentrate on the students' elocution. The story contains much conversation, which should be read with the same expression that the speakers used.

Discuss the difference between the two homes. One was lovely on the outside; the other had an inner beauty. Compare this with the differences in people's appearance. Often people we think are homely turn out to have a much more pleasant personality than those we think are beautiful or handsome. One reason may be that the person with a plain appearance tends to give more attention to developing character qualities, whereas the other one depends more on his looks to get ahead in life.

Help the students to realize that the inside is much more important than the outside, because the inside is what God considers. (See 1 Samuel 16:7.) Man judges by the outward appearance because that is as far as he can see.

Discuss the truth of Mrs. Olen's statement: "We have always had all we needed—enough to make us happy but not so much that it makes us discontented." Remind students that *things* can never make us happy. Have them try to recall instances of wanting something very badly; but when they got it, they soon discovered that it did not make them as happy as they thought it would.

You may want to discuss exercise 29 in class.

B. Reading for Comprehension .

21. The way we speak often tells something about us.

    a. What kind of voice did Mrs. Olen have when she called?   soft and shaky

    b. What kind of voice did Mrs. Ray have when she called?   snappy

22. Why did Lois look at her hands when she walked into the front room and Mrs. Ray screamed, "Don't drip that on that rug"?
    She thought something might be dripping from her hands.

23. Lois remained silent when the shaky clothes rod crashed to the floor and Mrs. Ray blamed her for it. But the story says, "There were things she could have said." What might Lois have said to Mrs. Ray?   Lois could have reminded Mrs. Ray that she herself had told Lois to
    put all the clothes on the rod when Lois was worried about it.

24. Write a sentence from the story that means about the same as the sentence below. "It seemed she wanted to tell Lois all about the Ray family."   Apparently she intended
    to thoroughly acquaint Lois with the Ray family before the day was over.

25. What word in Matthew 24:12 names what was missing in the Ray home?   love

26. What was the main reason that the Olen home did not look as drab to Lois after her first visit there as it had earlier? Circle the letter of the best answer.

    a. The sun was shining brightly the morning she arrived.

    b. The kitchen walls were colorfully painted.

    (c.) Love abounded in the Olen home.

27. The writer's purpose in this story is to teach that

    a. older people can love each other and be pleasant to work for.

    (b.) we should not judge only by outward appearance because it can be deceiving.

    c. beautiful houses are usually miserable homes.

28. Circle the letter of the verse that best matches the main idea of this story.

    a. "It is better to trust in the LORD than to put confidence in man" (Psalm 118:8).

    (b.) "Better is little with the fear of the LORD than great treasure and trouble therewith" (Proverbs 15:16).

    c. "And having food and raiment let us be therewith content" (1 Timothy 6:8).

105

Discussion Starters

1. In what way were the outward appearances of the two houses deceiving? (One house looked beautiful but was unpleasant within. The other house looked shabby but was pleasant within.)

2. a. Which house was the beautiful *house*? (the Rays' house)
   b. Which house was the beautiful *home*? (the Olens' house)
   c. Explain the difference between a beautiful house and a beautiful home. (A beautiful house is beautiful in appearance. A beautiful home has people who love each other.)

3. Why do you think Marianna enjoyed talking to Lois? (Lois spoke kindly to her and took an interest in what she said.)

4. What did Mrs. Olen mean when she said, "We have always had . . . enough to make us happy but not so much that it makes us discontented"? (She was thankful that they had the things they really needed. She realized that having too many things tends to make people dissatisfied.)

5. a. In what way was the Ray home poor? (The family members did not love each other even though they lived in a fine house.)
   b. In what way was the Olen home rich? (The husband and wife loved each other even though they lived in a shabby house.)

Fifth Reader Workbook

C. Writing for Comprehension

29. What did Mrs. Olen mean when she said that she was her husband's feet and he was her eyes?

Mr. Olen could not walk well, so Mrs. Olen did most of his walking. Mrs. Olen

could not see well, so he used his eyes to help her.

D. Review

30. What is a biography?   the story of a person's life

42. The Plough

By his choice of words in this poem, the writer helps us to form pictures in our mind of what he is describing. As you read the first stanza, you should picture the dark outline of a rounded hilltop set against the deep orange color of the sunrise. Above the orange is a streak of pale yellow blending into a thin line of deep blue.

But do not miss the deeper meaning of this poem. It refers to much more than the natural picture. These exercises should help you discover the lesson that the poet wanted to teach.

A. Defining for Comprehension

Complete sentences 1–6 with the following words, which are found in the poem.

somber (spelled **sombre** in the poem)   gilds
swell   ascends
hue   stalwart
beam   advance

1. After taking off, an airplane often ___ascends___ above the clouds.

2. The ___stalwart___ elephant blocked the path of the explorer and would not let him ___advance___.

3. With the sky so cloudy, the old stone house had a ___somber___ appearance.

4. The headlights of a car glowed over a distant ___swell___, or rounded hilltop.

5. A ___beam___ of sunlight ___gilds___ the western sky with its golden color.

6. The fresh, spring lawn had a beautiful green ___hue___.

7. Write the meaning of **colloquy**. ___conversation; dialogue___

8. Read the last two lines of stanza 2. What would be a simpler way of expressing the thought in these lines? Circle the letter of the best answer.
   a. The blackbird is a moody bird.
   (b.) The blackbird talks to himself.
   c. The blackbird is lonely.

9. Which pair of words below has the same thought as the phrases "stalwart horses" and "rigid ploughmen"? Circle the letter of the best answer.
   a. care and caution   (c.) purpose and perseverance
   b. vanity and vexation   d. danger and distress

10. What is another spelling for **plough**? ___plow___

107

Lesson 42

To the Teacher

Compare the rhyme and rhythm patterns of this poem with those in "God Is Love." Note that in both poems, the first and third lines rhyme as do the second and fourth lines. The rhythm patterns are opposite. Each line in "The Plough" begins with an unaccented syllable (iambic rhythm), whereas the lines in "God Is Love" begin with accented syllables (trochaic rhythm). The pattern in "The Plough" is like that in "Growing Smiles" (Lesson 21); however, the two poems have different line lengths.

Spend time discussing the beautiful imagery in this poem. (See exercise 13.) Be sure the students understand the meanings of the more difficult words.

Emphasize the thought expressed in the last stanza, and read Galatians 6:7–9 in relation to it. What we do today, and how we do it, will affect our future more than we realize.

This lesson requires much teacher involvement to make it worthwhile. Note that there is no part C; the students are to draw and color a picture instead.

Discussion Starters

1. How do you know this poem was probably written long ago? (The plowing was done with horses.)
2. How do you know the plowman got up early? (He was already working at dawn.)
3. What season of the year is it in the poem? (probably fall,

Fifth Reader Workbook

B. Reading for Comprehension

11. What does the poet advise the plowmen to think about as they work?_____

    They should remember that their labor is for the future.
    _____

12. This poem reminds us that life is serious. Our labor today is for future hours. As a young person, you must realize that the things you do today will have a very real effect on your future. If you plow "deep and straight" and sow good seeds in your youth, you may look forward to a rich harvest in the future.

    Circle the letters of the sentences below that give ways of plowing deep and straight.

    (a.) Learning math facts well so that you can work with numbers when you grow up.

    (b.) Obeying your parents promptly so that it will be easier to obey God.

    c. Doing all your work quickly so that you are always finished first.

    (d.) Being thoughtful of others all the time.

    e. Helping your parents so that you can go on a picnic.

13. Read again the introductory paragraph of this lesson. Then draw a sketch to illustrate the picture that the first stanza of the poem brings to your mind. Color the picture according to the colors suggested in the poem.
    (Grade according to the accuracy of the details.)

since the air is cold, all is silent except the blackbird, and the labor is not for the present but for future hours)
4. What is "nostril steam"? (vapor from the horses' nostrils)
5. Why should the plowman not look back as he plows? (He must look ahead to plow a straight furrow.)

C. Review for Test 7

14. Find and write a simile from the first stanza of the poem. __like yellow sand__

15. Tell whether each phrase below is a simile (**S**) or a metaphor (**M**).

    __S__ a. like a billowy cloud

    __M__ b. was a raging giant

    __M__ c. hooves were sledgehammers

    __S__ d. as sweet as honey

16. Give the meaning of each term.

    a. biography (Lesson 38) __story of a person's life__

    b. writer's purpose (Lesson 1) __author's most important reason for writing a story__

    c. imagery (Lesson 15) __word picture__

    d. rhythm (Lesson 21) __regular pattern of accented and unaccented syllables__

17. Be sure you know the meanings of the words in Defining for Comprehension, Lessons 37–42.

Fifth Reader Workbook

 43. The Laborers in the Vineyard

This is another parable that Jesus told to teach us a heavenly truth. In this story we get a glimpse of how workers were hired and paid in Bible times. A penny was a standard day's wage, even for a Roman soldier. It was a small silver coin also called a denarius.

A. Defining for Comprehension

1. This parable contains the word **householder** and the phrase **goodman of the house.** Both mean about the same thing. Circle the letter of the best definition for these terms.

   a. The father of a family.
   b. The owner of a house or property.
   c. The foreman at a job.

2. Write a word from the parable to match each definition.

   a. Not working; not busy. __idle__
   b. Manager; overseer. __steward__
   c. Worked; labored. __wrought__
   d. Endured; suffered. __borne__

3. The third paragraph has a word that means "the same thing." Later in the parable it is used with the meaning "also." What is this word? __likewise__

B. Reading for Comprehension

4. In Bible times, people considered 6:00 A.M. as the beginning of the day. So the first hour of the day was 7:00 A.M., the second hour was 8:00 A.M., and so on. Write the time for each of the following according to the system we use.

   a. __9:00 A.M.__ third hour   c. __3:00 P.M.__ ninth hour
   b. __12:00 noon__ sixth hour   d. __5:00 P.M.__ eleventh hour

5. Where did the husbandman go to hire workers? __to the marketplace__

6. Why were some still standing idle at the eleventh hour? __No one had hired them.__

7. Hired workers were paid at the end of each day. Why was this done? (See Leviticus 19:13.) __The Law of Moses did not allow a man to keep the wages of hired workers overnight.__

8. Who was paid first? __those who were hired last__

110

Lesson 43

To the Teacher

The parable of the laborers in the vineyard gives some excellent insight into the employment system of Jesus' day. Apparently, if a man needed help, he went to the marketplace to look for workers, and the men who were hired agreed to work for only one day at a time. A full working day consisted of about twelve hours, from sunrise to sunset.

The "penny" (denarius) of the New Testament was a silver coin about the size of an American dime. This was the standard wage for a day's work. Can the students think of other passages in which the penny (or pence) is mentioned? (See Matthew 18:28; Luke 7:41; 10:35; 20:24; John 12:5.)

Spend some time discussing the central truth that the parable teaches. Point out that this truth is the main reason for giving the parable, so not every detail applies to real life. For example, no one will grumble in heaven about the rewards that are given; but by this detail, Jesus was able to bring out the main truth He was teaching.

Also point out that it was through no fault of their own that some of the laborers worked only one hour. It appears that they would have worked all day if they had been hired in the morning, so the householder paid them a full day's wage.

You may need to discuss exercise 12 before assigning it. Help students understand the value of the New Testament penny by using a modern day's wage as a standard of comparison.

9. Why did some of the workers complain against the husbandman?_____

   __Every worker received a day's wage whether or not he had worked all day.__

10. Which is the main lesson that the parable teaches?

    a. We should work hard no matter what happens.

    b. God will reward all who serve Him faithfully.

    c. Employers should pay their workers promptly and fairly.

    d. Hired workers should not complain about their wages.

11. Copy the part of the last sentence in the parable that has this meaning: God asks many people to serve Him, but few people do so.

    __Many be called, but few chosen.__

C. Writing for Comprehension

12. Read Mark 6:34–37, noticing especially the phrase "two hundred pennyworth." Then write a paragraph explaining why the disciples must have thought that Jesus' command, "Give ye them to eat," was almost impossible to perform. The lesson introduction should help you.

    __(Explanation should include the idea that two hundred pennyworth was a big sum,__

    __equal to the wages of two hundred days.)__

D. Review

Choose from the following words to fill in the blanks.

biography, fiction, main idea, nonfiction, parable

13. A ____parable____ is an earthly story with a heavenly meaning.

14. A ____biography____ is the story of a person's life.

15. The ____main idea____ of a story is the most important truth or lesson in it.

16. An imaginary story is called ____fiction____.

Discussion Starters

1. What is a parable? (an earthly story with a heavenly meaning)

2. What is represented by the householder? The vineyard? The laborers hired earlier and later? (The householder represents God. The vineyard represents the world, or the place of service for Christians. The laborers hired earlier represent people who respond to God's call early in life and serve Him a long time. The laborers hired later represent people who respond to God's call later in life and serve Him only a short time, apparently because they do not hear the call until they are older.)

3. How do we know the workers trusted the householder when he hired them? (The householder simply promised to pay them "whatsoever is right," and they went to work for him.)

4. The owner of the vineyard is called by what three names? (householder, lord of the vineyard, goodman of the house)

Fifth Reader Workbook

 44. The Basketmaker of Cavan

There is a saying, "Give a man a fish, and he eats for a day. Teach him how to fish, and he eats for a lifetime." Today's story illustrates the truth of that saying. We do not always help people the most by giving them what they ask for. Sometimes we can help them more by encouraging them to think and work for themselves.

A. Defining for Comprehension

Complete these sentences with words from the list. You will not use all the words.

livelihood	charitable	anticipation
resolved	incident	native
encountered	prospect	invalids
perplexed	complied	ignorance

1. The young man __resolved__ to earn money by honest work.

2. Most people make their __livelihood__ by working for others.

3. The __prospect__ of finding gold lured many people to California in 1849.

4. Mr. Bailey __complied__ with the wishes of his landlord.

5. A strange __incident__ happened on our trip.

6. The __perplexed__ boy did not know where to find his parents.

7. William Penn, a __native__ of England, founded Pennsylvania.

8. The pioneers __encountered__ many problems as they settled in America.

9. Our class enjoyed singing for the two __invalids__.

10. Write sentences of your own, using the three leftover words in the list above.
    a. __(Individual sentences using *charitable, anticipation,* and *ignorance.*)__
    b. _____
    c. _____

11. Define the word **perseverance**. __keeping on in spite of difficulty__

B. Reading for Comprehension

12. Ned persevered in making __baskets__ and in translating __hymns (songs)__.

13. What was probably the main reason that Ned's family was poor? _____
    __Their father had died.__

112

Lesson 44

To the Teacher

Locate Ireland, in the British Isles, on a wall map.

Tell the students that this story took place before the days of machines and factories. At that time, things that we now take for granted had to be made individually by hand.

Discuss the wisdom Mrs. Farnham showed in having Ned work for money instead of giving it to him outright. There were two advantages in this: It taught Ned responsibility and the joy of labor, and it gave Mrs. Farnham something for her money.

Comment on Ned's perseverance, which had a very important part in his success both as a basketmaker and as a hymn translator. Also point out the interest that Mrs. Farnham

took in Ned. God usually brings blessings into our lives by using other people. Are we allowing Him to use us in this way? Do we respond to the help others give to us?

Point out that even though Ned's daughter never displayed her talent in public, it was still a great blessing and brought glory to God. In a similar way, our faithfulness in filling small places in God's kingdom can be a great blessing to others, even though very few people know about it.

Discussion Starters

1. Why is it better to work for a living than to have money handed to us? (Working develops our character and builds proper self-respect. We appreciate things we work for more than things that are handed to us.)

14. Why did Ned have to beg for a livelihood before Mrs. Farnham helped him? Circle the letter of the best answer.

    a. He was only fifteen and therefore not dependable.

    b. He was too lazy to work.

    c. People thought him undependable.

    d. For all the reasons above.

15. Mrs. Farnham asked Ned to make her a basket

    a. because she needed a basket badly.

    b. because she wanted a cheaper basket than she could buy elsewhere.

    c. because she wanted to help Ned.

    d. for all the reasons above.

16. How was the housekeeper different from Mrs. Farnham?

    a. The housekeeper was not as considerate as Mrs. Farnham.

    b. The housekeeper was not as charitable as Mrs. Farnham.

    c. The housekeeper was not as polite as Mrs. Farnham.

    d. In all the ways described above.

17. Why did making a basket for Mrs. Farnham give Ned a feeling of self-respect?

    a. He had succeeded at doing something hard but worthwhile.

    b. It was more honorable to work for money than to beg.

    c. He had proved that he could earn money by working.

    d. For all the reasons above.

18. In Part II of the story, what did Ned find time to do that shows he had an interest in spiritual things? reading the Bible

19. Which was harder for Ned to master, making baskets or translating songs into Gaelic? translating songs

20. How was Ned able to repay some of Mrs. Farnham's kindness to him? by translating her favorite hymns and singing them for her

21. How can we tell that Ned's daughter was not proud of her singing talent? She did not display her talent in public, but used it to cheer invalids and children.

2. What evidence is there that Ned would have been willing to work even before this? (He liked the idea of earning things rather than begging for them.)

3. Was Mrs. Farnham living in luxury? (No; she had enough money to live in pleasure, but she chose to live a plain and quiet life.)

4. How did Clarence show that he also had learned kindness? (When he saw Ned's clothes, Clarence wanted to give him some of his own clothes.)

5. Describe how Ned and his family surprised Mrs. Farnham. (Ned translated into Gaelic two French songs that were Mrs. Farnham's favorites. He taught the songs to his family, and then they sang the songs for Mrs. Farnham.)

6. Why do you think that Ned was never ashamed of being called Ned the Basketmaker? (Making baskets had helped to raise him from a life of poverty and begging to a life of usefulness and service to God.)

Fifth Reader Workbook

C. Writing for Comprehension

22. Explain how selling his first basket to Mrs. Farnham was a turning point in Ned's life.

    It taught Ned to earn a living by working rather than begging.

    This led to a lifetime of working for the good of others.

23. Tell what would probably have happened in Ned's life if Mrs. Farnham had simply given him money instead of starting him at making baskets.   (Sample answer.)

    Most likely he would have remained a beggar, unable to support his family. He may

    have started doing wrong things such as stealing, rather than serving God.

D. Review

24. Write whether each sentence is true (**T**) or false (**F**).

    T   a. **Wrought** means "worked; labored."

    T   b. **Borne** means about the same as **endured**.

    F   c. **Idle** and **busy** are synonyms.

45. Charley and Anna

Charley was a boy who had big ideas but had not stopped to consider how practical his plans were. He is an example of people in general who rush ahead with their own plans without stopping to consider God's will for their lives.

A. Defining for Comprehension

1. Write a definition for **citron.** Be sure your definition agrees with the way the word is used in the poem. _____

   a small, hard-fleshed watermelon used in pickles and preserves

2. Write a word from the poem for each of the following definitions.

   a. A dot; small spot. speck

   b. An inlet of the sea. bay

   c. Danger; risk. hazard

   d. Supplies; furnishes. provides

   e. Lets; allows. permits

   f. Hinders or stops. prevents

B. Reading for Comprehension

(Combined activities may be listed separately.)

3. List ten things that Charley planned to do when he saw that summer was coming.

   a. He planned to run in the fields.

   b. He planned to hear the birds sing and to sing himself.

   c. He planned to hunt up his kite and fly it.

   d. He planned to take his hoe and his cart to the garden.

   e. He planned to make a bed in the garden.

   f. He planned to plant watermelon and green citron seeds.

   g. He planned to keep the weeds out.

   h. He planned to get William to fix his boat.

   i. He planned to sail across the pond.

   j. He planned to gather flowers.

4. What is meant by the expression "castles of pleasure"? Circle the letter of the best answer.

   a. castles for doing pleasurable things

   b. pleasurable ambitions and daydreams

   c. thoughts of mischief

   d. plans for enjoyable work in the future

115

Lesson 45

To the Teacher

In the first part of the poem, we can readily picture Charley as being a daydreamer. Notice the expression "castles of pleasure"—the equivalent of "air castles." These phrases refer to people's dreams of things to be accomplished, which often sound grand but have little or no substance to them. Although not all dreaming is wrong, we must have a proper balance between dreaming and working. "Dreams belong to those who are willing to pay the price to make them come true."

Observe Anna's down-to-earth counsel. Pay special attention to the last three lines, which give the theme or main idea of the poem. Read James 4:13–15 to the pupils in connection with this. We do not know what the future holds, and it is only as the Lord wills that we can carry out our plans.

Literary concept in this lesson:

Theme (See exercise 6.)

Discussion Starters

1. What did Charley see that first inspired all his plans? (He saw the bright sun one morning as summer was coming.)
2. Is it wrong to plan what we want to do? (no)
3. What should we have in mind as we plan? (We may not be able to do the things we plan.)
4. Do you think Charley had kept the weeds out of his garden

Fifth Reader Workbook

5. Underline the best answers.

   a. Charley was probably about (5, <u>10</u>, 15) years old.

   b. Anna was probably about (5, 10, <u>15</u>) years old.

6. The *theme* of a composition is the same as its main idea. Both words indicate the main, general thought that a writer is presenting. Read James 4:13–15, which has the same theme as this poem. Then circle the letter of the statement below which best describes that theme.

   a. It is wrong to make plans for the future.

   b. We should not plan things unless we are sure we can do them.

   (c.) We should have a proper attitude about future plans.

7. Copy a verse from Proverbs 27 which has much the same thought as the first four lines that Anna spoke.   "Boast not thyself of to morrow; for thou knowest not what a day may bring forth" (Proverbs 27:1).

C. Writing for Comprehension

8. Tell how Anna's ideas were more mature than Charley's.   (Sample answer.) Anna understood that big plans do not always succeed. She said we should not be so sure about our plans, but look to God to prosper our way.

D. Review

Write whether each sentence is true (T) or false (F).

   _F_ 9. A native is a person from a foreign land.

   _T_ 10. Invalids are sick or disabled people.

   _F_ 11. **Resolved** and **determined** are antonyms.

   _F_ 12. To comply with something is to rebel against it.

   _T_ 13. **Anticipation** and **expectation** are synonyms.

   _T_ 14. "The Basketmaker of Cavan" is nonfiction.

   _T_ 15. A charitable person would be a helpful person.

116

in the past year? Explain. (No. He said, "This year, I am sure, I shall keep out the weeds," which suggests that he had failed to do that in the past.)

5. Who controls the things that come into our lives? (God)

46. Fifteen-barge Tow

Inland rivers and lakes are God-given highways on which man can move tremendous loads. A much greater quantity of goods can be hauled in a single load on water than on land. This makes it cheaper to use water transportation than most other kinds.

A. Defining for Comprehension

Match the definitions to the words from the story.

Part I

_d_	1. maneuvering	a.	Bin with sloping sides.
_c_	2. intercom	b.	Wrong name for something.
_f_	3. flexible	c.	Device for two-way communication.
_b_	4. misnomer	d.	Guiding from one place to another; steering.
_a_	5. hopper	e.	Black oil pumped from the ground.
_e_	6. petroleum	f.	Bending easily.

Part II

_q_	7. clearance	g.	In a friendly way; without showing ill will.
_i_	8. galley	h.	Having circuit boards, transistors, and so on.
_k_	9. counterpart	i.	Kitchen on a ship.
_o_	10. roger	j.	Area for off-duty crew members.
_l_	11. compensate	k.	Person who does the same job as another.
_p_	12. procedure	l.	Make up for; offset.
_n_	13. junction	m.	Exploring with something pointed.
_r_	14. pliant	n.	Place where two things join; meeting place.
_h_	15. electronic	o.	Word that means "I received your answer."
_m_	16. probing	p.	Method of doing something.
_g_	17. graciously	q.	Room to pass through.
_j_	18. quarters	r.	Bending easily.

Circle the letter of the best definition for these compound words from the story.

19. payload   (a.) Cargo or freight carried by a vehicle.
               b. Cargo to be paid for upon delivery.

Lesson 46

To the Teacher

As the pupils read this account orally, pause occasionally and ask questions to ensure that they are comprehending the progression of events. Explain that the barges were arranged in three rows with five barges in each row. Discuss the tremendous weight of this cargo. Point out that shipping heavy freight like this can be done more cheaply by water than by land because the water helps carry along the weight, and a much greater quantity of goods can be hauled at one time.

Sketch the fifteen-barge tow on the board. (This will help to prepare students for exercise 22.) Be sure they understand that the tow is the fifteen barges tied together.

On a wall map, trace the journey of the *Monarch* from Cincinnati, Ohio, to New Orleans, Louisiana. Compare this journey with the one described in "A Night on the Mississippi." In both accounts, cargo was carried down the Mississippi River toward New Orleans (though Lesson 19 does not mention a specific destination). In Lesson 19 it was done by two young boys on a simple raft, but in this lesson many tons of cargo are pushed by a towboat manned by a crew of experienced workers.

Draw a sketch of a lock on the board, explaining how it acts as a step to transfer boats between different water levels along a river. This relates to exercise 30.

Fifth Reader Workbook

20. radiophone   a. Telephone with a radio attached.
                (b.) Telephone for sending messages by radio waves.

B. Reading for Comprehension

21. On which river does the tow begin?   <u>Ohio River</u>

22. Draw a simple sketch of the fifteen-barge tow. Put the towboat at the right place, and draw an arrow to show in what direction it is moving.
(Sample sketch.)

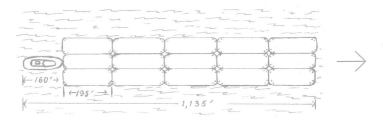

23. What cargo was carried on the fifteen-barge tow? _____
<u>grain, coal, railroad cars, combines, petroleum products</u>

24. a. How long was the towboat? <u>160 ft.</u>
    b. What was the length of one barge? <u>195 ft.</u>
    c. What was the total length of the fifteen-barge tow, including the towboat? <u>1,135 ft.</u>

25. Why were two-way radios needed on the tow? <u>The distance from one end to the other</u>
<u>was so great that the workers could not talk back and forth.</u>

118

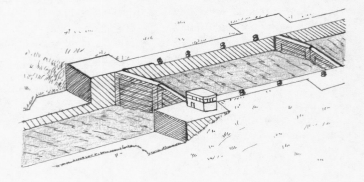

Discuss the dangers associated with the trip—especially the sandbars and low water level—and how each of these was a potential hazard to the *Monarch*.

Literary concept in this lesson:

Outlining a story plot (See exercise 29.)

Discussion Starters

1. Why did the pilot have a concerned look at the beginning of the story? (The water in the river was low.)
2. What simile is used to describe how the deck hands kept the ropes tight? ("like a cowboy bringing in a wild horse")
3. Why would the pilot want safety lines between all the

26. At what town does the Ohio River flow into the Mississippi?   Cairo, Illinois

27. What was the main reason this journey was taking longer than usual? _____

   The water level was low.

28. What accident happened as the tow came clear of a sandbar? _____

   A man fell overboard.

29. An **outline** is a list of the main ideas or events in the order they appear in a composition. Below is a partial outline of "Fifteen-barge Tow." Fill in the main events that are missing.

   a.   The towboat moved into the open channel of the river.

   b.   The tow was made up.

   c.   The tow started for New Orleans.

   d.   The tow passed through the first lock.

   e.   The tow ran onto a sandbar.

   f.   The tow reached the New Orleans harbor.

C. Writing for Comprehension

30. Write a paragraph explaining how a lock works. You might find information under "Canal" in an encyclopedia.   (Sample explanation.)

   A lock has two sets of gates. The first set opens to let a boat enter the lock. Then

   the gates close, and the water level is raised or lowered to the level of the water

   upstream or downstream. When the level is right, the other gates open and the

   boat goes on its way.

D. Review

Choose from the following words to fill in the blanks.

     biography, character, fiction, outline, parable

31. A   parable   is an earthly story with a heavenly meaning.

32. A   biography   is the story of a person's life.

33. The   outline   of a story gives the main events in the order they take place.

34. An imaginary story is called   fiction .

barges? (for extra safety in case one of the main snubbing ropes broke)

4. Why is *towboat* really a wrong name for the boat that powers a tow? (The towboat pushed the tow rather than pulling it.)

5. How did the pilot get the tow off the sandbar? (by shifting to full reverse and turning the rudder back and forth until the tow came clear)

6. Does the Mississippi River run in a straight line? How do you know? (No; the tow went around many S-curves, which one writer described as being in the shape of an apple paring thrown over one's shoulder.)

7. In the last paragraph, find four things that made this journey a challenge. (low water, winding rivers, sandbars, fog)

Fifth Reader Workbook

 47. The Other Half of the House

People are usually more convinced about the Gospel if they can see it lived out in the lives of true Christians. In this story, the Mansuetos were able to see that a true church was much more than a large building with a sad-faced statue in front.

A. Defining for Comprehension

1. The following words are used in the story. Write sentences of your own, using the words with the same meanings that they have in the story. (Words should have the meanings given.)
   a. variety   quality of having different parts; diversity
   b. scrambled   moved or climbed hastily
   c. wondering   being curious about
   d. polite   showing good manners

2. Write definitions for these words.
   a. breadfruit   tall, tropical tree of the mulberry family, or its melonlike fruit
   b. fiesta   religious holiday celebrated in a Spanish-speaking country
   c. cockfight   fight between gamecocks (roosters trained to fight)

B. Reading for Comprehension

3. About how many steps led up to the Mansueto side of the house? Read the first paragraph carefully to find out. Consider especially the step that Pepita was sitting on.   12 steps

4. Circle the letter of the word or phrase that best tells what the new neighbors' father was. Give proof of your choice with several details from the story. (Hint: What did he do?)
   a. schoolteacher
   b. missionary
   c. hymn writer
   d. salesman   (Sample details.)
   He invited people to church in his house.
   He prayed and preached. He went out to talk with people.

5. What was happening in church when everything became very still and then one voice spoke slowly?   The people were having prayer.

6. Carlos knew his mother was making excuses when she said that she could not go to the church next door because she had to keep Pedro. What was the real reason?   She was afraid to go to any church but the big one in the city. (or) She was afraid of what the priest would say.

120

Lesson 47

To the Teacher

This story takes place in the same general area as "The Oil or the Book." Point out that in both stories the house is built on stilts. Also, in both stories the children are more inclined to go to church than their parents are.

Compare the two concepts of a church expressed in this story. The Mansuetos thought of the church as a grand, elaborate building in the city. The newcomers spoke of *church* as the worship of God. Point out that a building can be called a church, worshiping God can be called church, and a group of believers who are faithful to God can be called a church.

Compare the Filipino custom of sharing houses with the North American practice of two families living in a duplex, or many families living in an apartment building.

Discussion Starters

1. Why was the house built above the ground, with a space under it? (In the Philippines and nearby tropical lands, many houses are built on stilts because of frequent flooding or simply because the ground is often wet. Pigs and chickens may live in the space underneath. To dispose of garbage, people simply drop it through cracks in the floor.)
2. Why did the children think they had misunderstood when the neighbor invited other people to church in his house? (They thought a church was a big building with a statue in front.)

7. The Mansueto children sometimes heard their parents "whispering together very seriously." What were they probably talking about? Circle the letter of the best answer.

   a. the church in the city
   b. attending church in the other half of the house
   c. whether or not the children liked the new church

8. The parents saw their children growing "happier, kinder, more quick to obey" as they attended their neighbors' church. Would the parents have been likely to start going to that church if the children had become more disobedient? Why or why not?

   No. If going to church had caused the children to behave worse, the parents would not have been interested.

9. Carlos later became a minister. What was one thing he especially remembered about his childhood?

   He would never forget how he had peeked through a thin wall into a room where a church with no building of its own worshiped God.

10. Circle the letter of the statement below that best describes the main teaching of this story.

    a. A lack of privacy is not always bad.
    b. People, not buildings, make up churches.
    c. Children can influence their parents to come to church.
    d. The best churches are small ones.

C. Writing for Comprehension

11. In what ways was the Mansuetos' house different from houses in North America?

    (Differences include the thin woven walls, the bamboo floor, and the stilts on which the house was built.)

12. You may have been surprised at the lack of privacy that the new family had in the other half of the house. It is generally best for families to have more privacy than the families in this story had. However, in this case something good happened because of it. Write a paragraph explaining how the lack of privacy helped the Mansuetos to start attending church.

    By being able to see the church services, the Mansuetos were convinced that this was true worship. They could also see and hear how their neighbors lived, which was a testimony of the Gospel they were presenting.

D. Review

13. Why would it be wrong to describe this story as fiction?

    This story is not fiction because it actually happened.

3. How was the lack of privacy helpful in this story? (The Mansuetos could see and hear what happened in the church services as well as in their Christian neighbors' home all week.)
4. Why were the children happier and kinder when they attended church? (because of the stories they heard and the songs they sang)
5. Why are big, fancy church buildings unnecessary? (It is not the building that makes a church, but people worshiping God.)

Fifth Reader Workbook

 ## 48. "Lean Not Unto Thine Own Understanding"

Whether young or old, we should learn to follow the instructions and advice of parents, teachers, and other trustworthy people. If we learn this while we are young, it will help us to avoid many troubles both now and later in life. Time after time we will find that we are not wise enough to make decisions by ourselves. "Be not wise in thine own eyes," but learn to accept the counsel of others.

Your teacher will discuss the lesson verse with you. Use the outline below to help you write several paragraphs about the verse "Lean not unto thine own understanding." Remember to think about what you want to write before you start. Then stick to your main idea.

I. People in the Bible who rejected good advice because they thought they had better ideas

II. People in the Bible who followed good advice

III. Results of following or not following good advice

Review for Test 8

1. Be sure you know the meanings of the vocabulary words in Lessons 43–48.

2. Be sure you know what these terms mean. The last two are from earlier lessons.

   theme (Lesson 45)

   outline (Lesson 46)

   fiction and nonfiction (Lesson 14)

   parable (Lesson 36)

122

Lesson 48

To the Teacher

Focus the discussion on our need to depend on God. People who are willing to accept advice from others are not as likely to make foolish mistakes as those who do not. Point out that we can receive much helpful advice from God's Word, and He also helps us through our parents and other adults. Discuss examples of people who did or did not heed good advice from others, such as Moses (Exodus 18:13–26) and Rehoboam (1 Kings 11:1–19). This will give the children some ideas for getting started on their compositions.

Be sure the students understand the writing assignment. Check the compositions for neatness as well as for content and sentence structure.

Discussion Starters

(Use these questions to help your students understand the verse. Do not make fifth graders feel personally responsible to seek advice. Their main responsibility is to follow it.)

1. Why should we not lean on our own understanding? (We do not have enough understanding and experience to make good decisions without help from others.)

2. How does God show us His way through our parents, teachers, and others? (God uses these people to teach us Bible truths and to serve as examples for us to follow.)

3. What are the results of taking good advice? (Things go better for us than if we just do what we think is best.)

49. The Very School of Snow

To experience a blizzard such as the author describes in this essay is truly awesome. It is another part of God's marvelous handiwork. Blizzards have the unique affect of drawing people together as they pool their efforts to recover from the storm.

A. Defining for Comprehension

1. Find a word in the second paragraph that means the opposite of **evergreen.** _deciduous_

2. The words below are used in the first seven paragraphs to describe the buildup of the storm. Some words have to do with the snow and some with the wind. Place the words under the correct headings in the order they are found in the essay.

gusts	whirls	pelt
shriek	fast falling	buffet
shot	puff	long, slanting lines
wavering	straight down	sauntering
turbulent	shrilly	

Snow	**Wind**
wavering	puff
sauntering	whirls
fast falling	gusts
straight down	turbulent
pelt	shrilly
shot	shriek
long, slanting lines	buffet

Match the following words and definitions.

_g_	3. reared	a.	Sharp or striking difference.
_b_	4. descent	b.	Falling action; downward motion.
_f_	5. grotesquely	c.	Overtaken by night.
_i_	6. solitude	d.	Slow-moving; unhurried.
_d_	7. leisurely	e.	Calls forth; arouses.
_h_	8. medley	f.	Strangely; unnaturally.
_j_	9. security	g.	Raised; brought up.
_a_	10. contrast	h.	Confused mixture.
_e_	11. summons	i.	Aloneness; isolation.
_c_	12. benighted	j.	Safety; protection.

13. The word **benighted** has a prefix and a suffix. What is the root word? _night_

Lesson 49

To the Teacher

Explain the meaning of the title. "The very school of snow" means "the very place to learn about snow." The author says this place is among the hills of western Connecticut.

Read the essay aloud to your students, using good expression. Help them see how the descriptive words in the third paragraph convey the mounting intensity of the storm. Point out how these words help them see, hear, and feel the effects of the storm. Note also the use of contrast between the cold, wild, stormy night outside and the warm, safe, comfortable living room.

Point out the frequent use of the words *like* or *as*. Remind

the students that these are the words used in similes. Explain that figures of speech help us to better visualize what is being described.

Call attention to the last sentence, which sums up the essay very aptly. Discuss why the author calls winter "the year's holiday," considering especially the time in which he lived. (Henry Ward Beecher, a Protestant minister, lived in 1813–87.)

You may want to discuss exercises 17 and 18 in class.

Discussion Starters

1. What details in the essay show that it was written a long time ago? (Horses and wagons were common. The fireplace was used for heat. There were no double windows; snow sifted in through the cracks. Villages could not

Fifth Reader Workbook

B. Reading for Comprehension

14. The words below are descriptive words found in the second paragraph. Study their context, and tell what they are describing.

    muffled   hides   clothed

    They describe the way snow covers things such as fences and trees.

15. Read Psalm 147:16. Both the psalmist and the writer of this essay compared snow to what?

    wool

16. One sentence contains these words: "Often the morning found scarfs of snow upon the bed." Is the figure of speech in this sentence a simile or a metaphor? _metaphor_

17. Explain why swamps could be entered safely and streams needed no bridges during a Connecticut winter in the author's childhood. _The swamps and streams were frozen over._

C. Writing for Comprehension

18. Near the end of the essay, the author describes how the whole neighborhood turned out to help open the roads. Write a paragraph telling how opening roads and highways today is different from long ago. Compare things such as the machinery used and the way people help each other.

    (Paragraph should mention modern snow removal equipment in contrast to the horses and shovels used long ago. People still help each other, but not nearly as much as in the 1800s.)

19. Tell why winter was "the year's holiday" to country people long ago.

    In winter there was no work such as plowing and planting, so the people had time for activities such as sleigh rides. They enjoyed traveling in all directions without being hindered by streams and fences. Shoveling snow gave them an opportunity to work together and enjoy each other's company.

D. Review

20. A paragraph that sums up the most important details of a story is a _summary_.

124

communicate with each other for several days. The people worked together to open the snowy roads. The young people went on sleigh rides.)
2. What is meant by "draw round the table" in the fifth paragraph? (Sit close together around the table.)
3. For what two reasons did the children pull the bed covers over their heads? (to deaden the sound of the storm and to keep out the snow)
4. Pick out the similes and metaphors in the essay. (Samples: "brought up in the very school of snow"; "[hidden] as by a mist"; "like a fog"; "[clothed] as with wool"; "scarfs of snow")

50. Cyrus McCormick Invents the Reaper

The invention of the reaper was a major step toward mechanized farming. This new machine helped to feed the world because it greatly increased the amount of grain that farmers could raise. Much patience and perseverance is required to produce a new invention, but it is God who gives men the raw materials and the ability to make such machines.

A. Defining for Comprehension

After each phrase below, write the word from the list that best matches it.

sickles	gristmills	hogsheads
scythes	smelting furnaces	vats

1. Fine wheat flour. **gristmills**

2. Barrels of water. **hogsheads**

3. Stooping to cut grain. **sickles**

4. Huge pans. **vats**

5. Iron ore. **smelting furnaces**

6. Standing to cut grain. **scythes**

B. Reading for Comprehension

7. Why did farmers of the early 1800s like to establish their farms along the banks of rivers? Circle the letter of the best choice.

   a. There were few roads at that time.

   b. The roads were rough and muddy.

   c. Rivers could be used to transport farm products to markets.

   d. For all the reasons above.

8. Copy a sentence from the third paragraph which suggests that Cyrus McCormick's great-grandfather was a farmer when he lived in Europe.

   "On this farm he plowed and harvested the grain with the farm tools he had brought with him from his home in Europe."

9. A *reference book* is a book for looking up information. Circle the letters of the two reference books that would be good places to look for a picture of a cradle scythe.

   a. encyclopedia   d. dictionary

   b. Bible dictionary   e. concordance

   c. atlas (book of maps)

125

Lesson 50

To the Teacher

Show the location of the Shenandoah Valley in Virginia on a map.

Contrast the hard, time-consuming labor of reaping by hand with the speed of the reaper and more modern equipment. Point out that for thousands of years, there was little change in the kind of farm implements used. In the past few centuries, however, automation and machinery have brought major advances in agriculture.

Discuss the difference between inventions and discoveries. (See Discussion Starters number 6.) You may wish to have the students write an essay on one major invention of the past two centuries. This would provide an opportunity for both writing and research.

Point out the importance of perseverance as exemplified in this story. Perseverance is needed not only to invent something but also to complete almost any task that we decide or are assigned to do. Help the pupils understand that every major accomplishment requires a great deal of effort behind the scenes. Be careful not to glorify man, however, but the Lord who gives man the ability to invent things.

Literary concept in this lesson:

Reference books (See exercise 9.)

Fifth Reader Workbook

10. In the sentence below, underline the word that helps us understand the meaning of **cradled.**
"These fingers cradled, or <u>held</u>, the grain until the knife had finished its work; then they laid it in neat rows to one side."

11. An invention is a new device that was never made before, such as the reaper in this story. A discovery is something man learns about that was unknown before. Write whether each of the following was an invention (**I**) or a discovery (**D**).

<u>I</u> a. steam engine   <u>D</u> e. gravity

<u>I</u> b. telephone   <u>I</u> f. computer

<u>D</u> c. solar system   <u>I</u> g. airplane

<u>D</u> d. electricity   <u>I</u> h. light bulb

12. Many machines invented since the reaper have benefited farmers. What is the name of a machine that combines the reaper's work of mowing grain and the threshing machine's work of threshing grain? (Hint: A form of the name appears in the question.) <u>combine</u>

13. From what this story says about McCormick's reaper, what was its main advantage? What was its main disadvantage? (Consider its performance in Farmer Ruff's field.) Answer both questions in one sentence.

<u>Its main advantage was speed, and its main disadvantage was that it did not work well on rough land.</u>

C. Writing for Comprehension

14. Write a simple, one-paragraph summary of this story. Your summary should tell what was invented, who invented it, when it was invented, where it was invented, and why it was invented. (Teacher: You may want to discuss these main points before assigning this exercise.)

<u>What: the reaping machine</u>

<u>Who: Cyrus Hall McCormick</u>

<u>When: near the beginning of the 1800s</u>

<u>Where: Virginia (Shenandoah Valley; in the Blue Ridge Mountains)</u>

<u>Why: to speed up the grain harvest and prevent loss due to weather</u>

D. Review

*Write whether each sentence is true (**T**) or false (**F**).*

<u>F</u> 15. A deciduous tree is an evergreen.

<u>T</u> 16. A summary is a paragraph that sums up the most important details of a story.

126

Discussion Starters

1. In the early 1800s, what products did farmers use in trading? What did they trade them for? (They used corn, wheat, flax, and wool. They traded these things for salt, iron, tea, tools, and other things.)
2. Why did the McCormick son start a farm along the Shenandoah River in Virginia? (Here he could have plenty of land for nothing.)
3. Why did everyone have to help at harvest time? (The harvest season was short, and all the work was done by hand.)
4. What is the difference between a scythe and a sickle? (A scythe is a large cutting tool with a long handle, and a sickle is a small cutting tool with a short handle.)
5. What was wrong with the first harvesting machine that the McCormicks made? (It trampled down the grain instead of cutting it.)
6. What is the difference between an invention and a discovery? (An invention is a new device that was never made before. A discovery is something man learns about that was unknown before.)

51. It Is Common

It is the things most familiar to us that we tend to take for granted. But as we count our blessings, we soon realize that we have much to be thankful for. Let us praise "the living God, who giveth us richly all things to enjoy" (1 Timothy 6:17).

A. Defining for Comprehension

1. Find a synonym in the poem for each of these words.

   a. glimmering ___glistening___

   b. joyfulness ___mirth___

   c. liberal ___generous___

   d. winding ___meandering___

   e. brooks ___rills___

2. Find an antonym in the poem for each of these words.

   a. frowns ___smiles___

   b. autumn ___spring___

   c. hate ___love___

   d. ugly ___beautiful___

   e. tame ___wild___

   f. none ___all___

3. The word **common** has several different meanings. Before each sentence below, write the number of the best definition for **common** as used in that sentence.

   1. Shared by everyone in a group.
   2. General; widespread.
   3. Familiar; usual.
   4. Ordinary; not of high class.
   5. Inferior; of poor quality.

   _4_ a. The common people heard Jesus gladly.

   _2_ b. Today it is common knowledge that the earth is round.

   _5_ c. The house was built of such common materials that it soon needed repair.

   _1_ d. In some countries, the whole family eats from a common bowl at mealtimes.

   _3_ e. Washing dishes is one of our most common household chores.

127

Lesson 51

To the Teacher

This is a good poem for oral reading. Be sure the students use good expression. Note the deep feeling in the poem, as well as the vivid word pictures.

Discuss the thought presented in the poem. Common things are often taken for granted, yet they would be sorely missed if we did not have them anymore. Indeed, we should bless the Lord that they are common.

Consider that these things are not common to everyone. Blind people cannot enjoy the sights described in the poem; those who live in deserts seldom hear "the rain with its pattering feet"; and many people in the world do not have "the bread which we daily eat."

Discuss the rhyme and rhythm patterns of the poem. Note that the last words in each pair of lines rhyme, and that the first, fourth, and fifth stanzas each have an extra line. The first syllable in each line is accented, followed by two unaccented syllables, as shown below.

/ ᴗ ᴗ / ᴗ ᴗ / ᴗ /
So are the stars and the arch-ing skies
/ ᴗ ᴗ / ᴗ ᴗ / ᴗ /
So are the smiles in the chil-dren's eyes;

Fifth Reader Workbook

4. The sentence above the poem says that it was written by an anonymous American poet. What is the meaning of **anonymous**? <u>not known; not named; not identified</u>

B. Reading for Comprehension

5. Poets often use special wording to express their thoughts. Consider the phrase "smiles in the children's eyes." What kind of eyes have smiles in them? Circle the letter of the best answer.

   a. clear blue eyes
   (b.) eyes that display happiness
   c. eyes that are slightly curved

6. Copy the expression that tells how rain sounds. <u>with its pattering feet</u>

7. If we are truly thankful for the many things God gives us, we will appreciate the common things in life rather than complaining about them. Write **X** before each quotation that suggests a proper attitude about common things.

  <u>X</u>   a. "Thank God for water."

  <u>   </u>   b. "This old pen still works, but I want a new one like Jane's."

  <u>   </u>   c. "Oh, no! More peas to pick."

  <u>X</u>   d. "I'll wash my hands first because I don't want to soil this book."

  <u>X</u>   e. "I'll use the back side of this paper to do my math calculations."

  <u>X</u>   f. "Look at the beautiful sunset God has made!"

  <u>   </u>   g. "Not potatoes for supper again!"

C. Writing for Comprehension

8. Write a paragraph telling about five things you have that you are thankful for. Try to think of things that the poem does not mention.

<u>(Individual paragraphs.)</u>

_____

_____

_____

_____

_____

128

Discussion Starters

1. Why is the breath of spring called life-giving? (It helps to bring new plants to life.)
2. Name other common blessings that the poem does not mention. (Sample answers: clouds, flowers, clothing, houses, health, five senses, the Bible)
3. Why is the harvest moon described as generous? (It gives an abundance of light. It is associated with a generous harvest.)
4. How is the hope of heaven common to all? (All who meet the conditions can go to heaven.)
5. What is the chorus of this poem? ("Blessed be God, it is common.")

52. The Fox Den

God gave His creatures many ways to defend themselves. Especially intriguing are the methods that some animals use to lure their enemies away from their young. Surely our God is a wise God.

A. Defining for Comprehension

After each sentence below, write a word from the following list to replace the underlined part. You will not use all the words.

versions	troupe	sensitive
concealed	outcry	abruptly
brook	distributed	gesture
glimpse	devoured	folly
discreetly	secluded	

1. Charles stopped his work <u>suddenly and unexpectedly</u>.   **abruptly**

2. The chickens made a <u>great noise</u> when they saw the weasel.   **outcry**

3. A bird's nest was <u>hidden from view</u> among the rushes and leaves.   **concealed**

4. The cottage stood in a <u>separate and hidden</u> part of the forest.   **secluded**

5. Allen quickly <u>handed out</u> all the song sheets that he had.   **distributed**

6. The hogs <u>gobbled up</u> every bit of their breakfast.   **devoured**

7. A lovely <u>small stream</u> wound its way through the hills.   **brook**

8. A wolf's ears are <u>able to hear very slight sounds</u>.   **sensitive**

9. Father's <u>expressive motion</u> clearly meant that we should be quiet.   **gesture**

10. A <u>small company</u> of persons was searching for the lost child.   **troupe**

11. Sheryl got only a <u>quick view</u> of the bird.   **glimpse**

12. We heard several <u>forms with slight differences</u> of the same story.   **versions**

B. Reading for Comprehension

How well did you concentrate? Circle the letters of the best answers for exercises 13–17 without looking back at the lesson. Then look back and correct any wrong answers.

13. In what time of the year does this story take place?
    a. autumn   (b.) spring   c. winter

14. What was the author doing when he found the fox den?
    (a.) watching birds build a nest
    b. watching birds feed their young
    c. watching a bird that tried to lure him from her nest

Lesson 52

To the Teacher

Discuss the God-given instinct of the fox in caring for her young, as illustrated by her craftiness and the fact that she always gave the best of her hunting to her young. Comment also on the excellent means the fox has of communicating danger to its young, and on their swiftness in responding. Ask the pupils what would have happened if the cubs had continued playing a few minutes longer, as children sometimes do.

You may wish to have the students do additional research on the habits of foxes, using an encyclopedia or some other reference book.

Discussion Starters

1. What games did the fox cubs play? (hide-and-seek, tag, "king of the castle," and several without names)
2. What different things did the mother fox do to try to catch the author's attention? (She came trotting as if she did not see the author. She turned her back and scratched an ear with a hind foot. She opened her mouth in a wide yawn. She began to bark or yap at him.)
3. When did the mother fox hunt food for her family? (at night)
4. How would a hound dog help you find a fox den? (by using his sense of smell)

Fifth Reader Workbook

15. What did the author think was the favorite food of the cubs?
    a. birds   b. fish   (c.) mice

16. How did the mother fox warn her cubs of danger?
    a. by giving a short bark
    b. by running in circles
    (c.) by pointing her ears at them

17. How does a mother fox carry her cubs?
    (a.) as a cat carries a kitten
    b. on her back
    c. by their tails

Answer these questions.

18. What was the mother fox trying to do when she seemed to be saying, "Here I am; catch me if you can"? _____
    She was trying to lure the author away from her den.

19. What is another name for a mother fox? __vixen__

20. Into what three parts is a young fox's day divided? _____
    eating, sleeping, playing

C. Writing for Comprehension

21. Explain why the mother fox made a circle of tracks around the den and playground when she heard a dog barking. _____
    She hoped the dog would follow the tracks and stay away from the den.

22. If you want to observe a mother fox and her cubs, why must you be careful not to leave your scent close to the den? The mother fox is likely to move the cubs if she detects your scent near the den more than once.

23. Why would a small dog be foolish if it tried to follow the mother fox into a small crevice in the rocks? _____
    The dog would get his nose nipped by the fox's sharp teeth.

D. Review

Write whether each sentence is true (T) or false (F).

__F__ 24. An invention is something man learns about that was unknown before.

__F__ 25. **Security** and **loneliness** are synonyms.

__T__ 26. A turbulent stream would have rushing water.

5. What do foxes do on a stormy day? (They sleep all day.)
6. How many circular paths did the cubs play on? (three)

53. The Answer for Niklaus

We are easily influenced by the actions of people around us. We may wonder, "Should I do what they are doing? Would that be better than what I am doing now?" In this story, Niklaus found happiness through accepting his place in life.

A. Defining for Comprehension

The sentences below are based on sentences in the story. Write the correct words from the list in the blanks after the sentences. Do not look back at the story until you have completed this exercise. You may use a dictionary if you need help.

chasm	scurried	attended
musings	unwary	reverberated
severe	ascent	clambered
immense	torrent	exhilarating
vigorously	stunned	descended
glaciers	treacherous	reassurance

1. Maria nodded her head ___ and ran back inside. _____ vigorously
2. The cows turned onto the trail and began the ___ up the mountain. _____ ascent
3. Niklaus and Maria ___ school during winter. _____ attended
4. Snowcaps and ___ topped the peaks that rose from the valley floor. _____ glaciers
5. "Why should we wear ourselves out here in these ___ mountains?" _____ treacherous
6. What would life be like without the ___ air of the heights? _____ exhilarating
7. It was possible to fall off a cliff and into a rocky ___ in the mountains. _____ chasm
8. A person could also fall into a rushing ___ far below. _____ torrent
9. A ___ storm was raging on the mountaintops, in spite of the pleasant day. _____ severe
10. Niklaus thought of the ___ columns of ice suspended at glacier edges. _____ immense
11. These columns were ready to topple onto ___ travelers. _____ unwary
12. Niklaus was glad to be drawn from his unpleasant ___ by a marmot. _____ musings
13. A feeling of ___ came over him as he repeated the line from the psalm. _____ reassurance
14. The notes ___ among the mountains to mark the end of the day. _____ reverberated

B. Reading for Comprehension

15. Circle the letters of three words which suggest that the setting of this story is Switzerland. A dictionary may help you decide.
    a. alligator   (d.) chalet
    (b.) cowbells   e. prairie
    c. oil fields   (f.) alp

Lesson 53

To the Teacher

Locate Switzerland on a map. Point out the location of the Alps in the southern and eastern parts of the country. Explain that the lower slopes of the Alps have grassy pasture land. For many years, people have made their living on these slopes by dairying.

Discuss the question Niklaus was facing. Point out that Niklaus was not so much trying to judge the actions of Franz's family as he was trying to answer the questions that their move raised in his own mind.

Focus the main part of the discussion on the rightness or wrongness of the move that Franz's family made to the city.

Students should see that it is not morally wrong to live in a city. A person's reasons for moving to the city need to be considered. The reasons given by Franz's father do not seem entirely sound, yet we cannot judge them as being wrong on the basis of the information given. Maybe he had back problems or a bad leg, which would have been a great hindrance to making a living as a farmer in the mountains.

On the other hand, although it is good that Niklaus loved the mountains, point out that a person sometimes loves his home so much that he is unwilling to leave it even for right reasons. The main factor in deciding whether we should move or stay, of course, should always be the Lord's will for our lives.

Fifth Reader Workbook

16. The Alps are a mountain range in Europe. What does the word **alp** mean?

   a high mountain

17. Why did Franz's father want to leave the Alps and move to the city? _____

   He thought life in the Alps was too hard and dangerous.

18. List three dangers that cowherds faced in the Alps.

   Falling into rocky chasms or rushing torrents.

   Becoming lost in a snowstorm or dense fog.

   Being crushed by falling glaciers or buried in a snow slide.

19. The title of the story is "The Answer for Niklaus."

   a. What question was Niklaus asking? _____

   Why would Franz's family want to leave the Alps? (Would it make life easier?)

   b. What was his answer? _____

   Niklaus decided not to leave the Alps.

20. The *title* of a story should be short and interesting. It should hint at the main idea but not give away the outcome of the story. Below are three other titles for this story. Circle the letter of the one that is best.

   a. Herding Cows in the Alps
   b. Niklaus Decides to Continue Herding Cows in the Alps
   c. A Puzzle for Niklaus

C. Writing for Comprehension

21. Near the end of the story, Niklaus "suddenly felt very sorry for his friend." Explain why Niklaus felt sorry for Franz.

   He felt sorry for Franz because he was leaving the beautiful mountains for life in the city.

22. What are three advantages of living in the country rather than living in the city?
   (Sample answers.)

   The country usually has fewer bad influences than the city.

   The country has plenty of room to work and play.

   The country usually has fresh air and beautiful scenery.

   Children in the country can usually work more closely with their parents.

132

Literary concept in this lesson:

Story titles (Discuss exercise 20 in class.)

Discussion Starters

1. What did Niklaus's family do with the milk from their cows? (They used it to make cheese.)
2. What was another activity in the high pastures besides herding cattle? (cutting and storing hay)
3. What things show that Niklaus loved his family? (He spoke cheerily to his mother as he started up the mountain. He picked flowers for Maria.)
4. What three things did Niklaus especially enjoy in the mountains? (the gentle cows, the rich pastures, and the exhilarating air)
5. What did Niklaus like about seeing the marmot? (It distracted him from his unpleasant musings.)
6. How did thinking about the Bible verse help Niklaus? (It brought a feeling of reassurance. He realized that city life could never be as peaceful as his life in the mountains.)
7. What sentence shows how the mountains made Niklaus feel? ("Now they seemed to smile down at him in a friendly, protective way.")

54. With Wings As Eagles

Sometimes our bodies grow tired and our spirits weary. But God never becomes tired, and He gives strength to those who serve Him in faith.

A. Defining for Comprehension

Write a word from this Bible passage for each of the following definitions.

1. Makes greater; adds to. __increaseth__

2. Completely; totally. __utterly__

3. Refresh; restore. __renew__

4. Rise; ascend; climb. __mount__

B. Reading for Comprehension

For exercises 5 and 6, give the numbers of the lines.

5. God is infinite, which means He is boundless and eternal. Which line of the poem says that?

   __line 2__

6. God is incomprehensible, which means He can never be fully understood. Which line of the poem says that?   __line 5__

This passage from Isaiah is another example of Hebrew poetry, with its "rhyming thoughts." For numbers 7–9, copy the two parallel lines that express the thought given in each statement.

7. Even men who are not old will become tired.

   __Even the youths shall faint and be weary,__

   __And the young men shall utterly fall.__

8. God strengthens those who are weak.

   __He giveth power to the faint;__

   __And to them that have no might he increaseth strength.__

9. They will travel by foot without becoming tired.

   __They shall run, and not be weary;__

   __And they shall walk, and not faint.__

133

Lesson 54

To the Teacher

Read this selection aloud to the class, using good expression.

Discuss the lesson contained in the passage. The selection portrays God as being omnipotent. He will give power to those who have the faith and patience to wait upon Him.

This passage also has a lesson for you, the teacher. Wait upon the Lord; draw strength from Him; and you will find yourself facing each morning with strength to mount up as eagles.

Give opportunity for students to ask questions that they might have.

Discussion Starters

1. Give three names used for God in this lesson. (the everlasting God, the Lord, the Creator)
2. What are some things that make us feel faint, as if we have no strength? (hard work, a big job to do, fear, and worry)
3. How can we fly up with wings like an eagle when we wait on God? (We let God take care of our troubles instead trying to deal with them in our own strength.)

Fifth Reader Workbook

Use the following poetry for exercises 10 and 11.

If we will serve the Lord our God,
Our fail-ing strength He will <u>re-store</u>.
And then as ea-gles we can rise
To live in tri-umph <u>ev-er-more</u>.

10. Which stanza of "With Wings As Eagles" has much the same thought as this poetry?

    stanza 3 (the last stanza)

11. This poetry has both rhyme and rhythm. Underline the rhyming words. Mark the syllables with / and ∪ to show the rhythm pattern.   (See markings above.)

C. Writing for Comprehension

12. In one or two sentences, give the meaning of the poem above. This is the main lesson we can learn from "With Wings As Eagles."

    This poem teaches that our mighty God gives power to those who serve Him. With

    this power, we can face hard things in life without falling.

D. Review for Test 9

13. Be sure you know the meanings of the vocabulary words in Lessons 49–54.

14. Write numbers to match the sentence beginnings and endings.

    4 a. A summary   1. should be short and interesting.
    5 b. To read for details 2. is a regular pattern of accented and unaccented syllables.
    1 c. A story title   3. is a pattern of matching sounds.
    3 d. Rhyme   4. is a paragraph that gives the main facts in a story.
    2 e. Rhythm   5. is to read with close attention in order to find facts.

55. Brother David's Song

This story teaches an important principle: respect for the elderly. Younger people have much to gain if they take time to sit down and listen to the wisdom of aged Christians. Elderly people greatly appreciate when youth and children take time to visit them and help them.

A. Defining for Comprehension

Match these words and definitions. If you need help, see how the words are used in the story.

_i_	1. beckoned	a.	Went along with.
_c_	2. consented	b.	Happening often; regular.
_h_	3. auditorium	c.	Agreed; gave approval.
_a_	4. accompanied	d.	Given little attention; forgotten.
_g_	5. elderly	e.	Asked; questioned.
_j_	6. tremulous	f.	Something picked out; choice.
_f_	7. selection	g.	Aged; old.
_e_	8. inquired	h.	Large room where listeners sit.
_d_	9. neglected	i.	Summoned with a gesture; motioned.
_b_	10. frequent	j.	Trembling; unsteady.

11. Write the phonetic spelling and the definition of **senile**. _(sē′ nīl), showing deterioration_ _of mind and body resulting from old age_

B. Reading for Comprehension

12. Brother David was forgetful because of his old age. In what two ways is this shown in the story? _He forgot the girls' names and faces._ _He wanted to sing the same song over and over._

13. One sentence mentions Brother David's "time-dulled ears." What does this tell about him? _He was hard of hearing._

14. Why did Jill like the tone of Brother David's voice as he sang the last phrase of his favorite hymn? Circle the letter of the best answer.

   a. His voice trembled as he sang.
   (b.) He sang with joy and confidence.
   c. His voice sounded like a child's.

Lesson 55

To the Teacher

Focus discussion on exercise 18. Respecting and visiting our grandparents is a means of maintaining the family unit. Society is suffering much from the breakdown of the family. In much the same way that every member of the church contributes to the increase and edification of the congregation, every member of a family supplies something needful. Godly grandparents can make a tremendous contribution to the spiritual well-being and edification of their children, grandchildren, and great-grandchildren. They should always receive our respect and devotion. This is also true of other elderly people among us, whether or not they are our relatives.

Discussion Starters

1. How can you tell at the beginning of the story that Jill had a proper respect for her parents? (She waited patiently for Mother's attention instead of interrupting her conversation.)
2. How did Sister Rhoda and the girls show respect for Brother David? (by visiting him, by speaking clearly, by asking him to suggest songs, by singing his favorite song repeatedly)
3. What would have happened if the girls had told Brother David that they had already sung his choice? (They would have made him feel bad. He might not have wanted to suggest any more songs.)

Fifth Reader Workbook

15. Jill noticed that Brother David had not forgotten his hope of former years. What was this hope?

   the hope of heaven

16. In what way was the girls' visit to Brother David a lesson in patience?   They had to be

   patient with his forgetfulness. They patiently sang the same song over and over.

17. What words would describe the character of girls who are willing to sing the same song five times for an elderly person? Underline all the correct words below.

   <u>humble</u>   selfish   proud   <u>polite</u>   <u>considerate</u>
   <u>respectful</u>   <u>patient</u>   <u>understanding</u>   careless   rude

C. Writing for Comprehension

18. A verse near the end of Leviticus 19 is a command to respect old people. Copy this verse.

   "Thou shalt rise up before the hoary head, and honour the face of the old man, and

   fear thy God: I am the LORD" (Leviticus 19:32).

19. After being introduced to Jill, Brother David said, "My own grandchildren are so busy, they don't very often have any time for me." It is sad when people have no time for their grandparents. It is something we must guard against. Write a paragraph telling why it is important to take time for our grandparents.   (Sample points are given.)

   We should respect our grandparents.

   Grandparents appreciate visits from their grandchildren.

   Grandparents can become lonesome or discouraged if no one visits them.

   We can benefit from the wisdom and experience of our grandparents.

   We may be able to help them by running errands.

   The Bible tells us to honor parents and respect old people.

136

4. How do you know that Brother David was eager to go to heaven? (He especially enjoyed songs such as "When the Roll Is Called Up Yonder" and "Safe in the Arms of Jesus.")

5. Why were the girls so happy on their way home? (They had been patient with Brother David and had been a blessing to him.)

56. Language Without *Love*

Think for a moment how it would be if the very idea of writing were unknown! Being able to read and write is certainly a great gift.

This story is also a lesson in perseverance. Think of how these missionaries persevered through their seemingly hopeless task until they could witness hundreds of people being delivered from their evil ways and living for God.

A. Defining for Comprehension

Match these words from the story with their definitions.

  _b_   1. enterprise   a. Not advanced in civilization

  _f_   2. colleagues   b. Project; undertaking

  _a_   3. primitive   c. Not working; idling

  _h_   4. pantomimes   d. Changes; adjustments

  _d_   5. modifications   e. Highly expressive; vivid

  _g_   6. nonexistent   f. Fellow workers

  _c_   7. loitering   g. Having no being; absent

  _e_   8. eloquent   h. Actions without speech

Write the expressions that Hensey and his fellow laborers used for the following words when they translated the Bible into Mongo-Nkundo.

9. snow   egrets

10. wolves   leopards

11. desert   dry country

12. steps   short up-paths

13. three-story houses   three-houses-high

14. candlestick   holder-of-torches

15. tents   cloth houses

16. window   small door

137

Lesson 56

To the Teacher

Show the students the location of the Congo River in west-central Africa. The nation usually called Congo was known as Zaire (zä ir′) for a time, but in 1997 it was renamed the Democratic Republic of the Congo.

Discuss the misunderstanding caused by Hensey's using his finger to point at things. Observe that even a gesture as "universal" as pointing is worthless when there are differences in custom. Hensey's perseverance in spite of such obstacles is highly commendable. In connection with this, you might also refer to the perseverance of those who translated the Bible into English—John Wycliffe, William Tyndale, Miles Coverdale, and others.

The whole enterprise described in the story is one of outstanding dedication and perseverance. Where would we start learning a language if we had no teacher and no books—indeed, if the very concept of writing were foreign to the speakers of the language? Hensey had at least four monumental objectives to achieve: (1) to learn the Mongo-Nkundo language, (2) to devise a system of writing for the language, (3) to translate the Bible into Mongo-Nkundo, and (4) to teach the people how to read. Observe the systematic method by which the missionaries attained each of these objectives. Also note the various keys that Hensey and his colleagues discovered by accident or chance, which helped to advance their labors—such as when they learned the true meaning of *bosai*.

Fifth Reader Workbook

B. Reading for Comprehension

17. Like any other North American or European, Hensey used his finger to point at things when he asked what they were called.

    a. What is the Mongo-Nkundo word for **finger**?   bosai

    b. How did the Mongo-Nkundo people point at something? _____

       They stuck out their lower lip at it.

18. Write the meaning of the word that Hensey finally discovered, which he used for **love.**_____

    caring so much that it hurts

19. The chief who visited Hensey while he was writing a letter became angry when Hensey said that he would send his words far away. In what three ways did the chief show his anger?

    He banged his tribal stick on the floor.

    His black eyes rolled.

    His nostrils widened.

20. Why did the chief use a stick to carry the paper that Hensey gave him? _____

    The chief was afraid to touch the paper.

21. How long was it from the time that Andrew Hensey began asking "Onka na?" until the New Testament was printed in Mongo-Nkundo?   15 years

C. Writing for Comprehension

22. Explain how Hensey went about finding the words for verbs such as **sitting** and **running,** and for adverbs such as **slow** and **fast.**

    Hensey performed the actions of the verbs, such as sitting and running, and asked

    the Africans to tell him the verbs. He performed the actions in different ways to get

    the adverbs.

23. Explain why the angry chief never got his six oranges. _____

    He was so terrified by the talking paper that he forgot about the oranges and ran to

    tell his people.

138

Point out that these happenings were directed by the providential hand of God.

    Consider the conclusion of the story. We can hardly imagine Hensey's feelings as he listened to a Christian hymn being sung by people who had been in the darkness of heathenism only twenty years earlier. Surely he felt amply rewarded for every day that he had devoted in service to these people.

Discussion Starters

1. Where does the story take place? (near the Congo River in central Africa)
2. Why was it a serious matter for the missionaries when it seemed that every word was *bosai?* (They were trying to learn the people's language.)
3. Why do you suppose the people called Hensey Grandfather? (They probably considered him wise.)
4. What was Henry's method of teaching letters long before slates or paper arrived? (He used a stick to write in the dust.)
5. Name all the things you can think of that show Hensey's perseverance. (Sample answers: He found out the names of trees, animals, and birds. He did pantomimes to get verbs and adverbs. He did much traveling in search of new words. He preached and told Bible stories. He translated the Bible into Mongo-Nkundo. He taught the people to read and write.)

57. Sleep Sweet

Peaceful rest is a gift of God to those who trust in Him. It is God who continually watches over His people.

A. Defining for Comprehension

1. What is a garish light? __a bright, glaring light__

2. Why do we like soft lights at night? __Soft lights are more calm and relaxing.__

B. Reading for Comprehension

3. This poem would make a good motto to hang in which room of the house? __bedroom__

4. Psalm 121 tells us that God keeps His people and never sleeps. We read this in verses __3__ and __4__.

5. Write a sentence describing the mood of this poem. There are two words in the first stanza that could be used in describing the mood.

   __The mood of this poem is quiet and peaceful.__

6. Copy the two lines that tell us not to let sad things of the past disturb our rest.

   __And let no mournful yesterdays__

   __Disturb thy peaceful heart.__

7. Copy the two lines that tell us not to let worries about the future keep us from sleeping.

   __Nor let tomorrow mar thy rest__

   __With dreams of coming ill.__

C. Writing for Comprehension

Make a simple motto of this poem to hang in your bedroom. Your teacher will direct you.

D. Review

*Write whether each sentence is true (**T**) or false (**F**).*

__T__ 9. A colleague is a fellow worker.

__T__ 10. **Utterly** means "totally" or "completely."

__F__ 11. To keep something from changing is a modification.

__T__ 12. The story "Language Without *Love*" took place in Africa.

139

Lesson 57

To the Teacher

Read this poem orally to the class, conveying a calm and restful mood. In talking about its content, note that the first stanza tells us not to grieve about the past, and the second stanza tells us not to worry about the future.

You may wish to read Psalm 121 in connection with this poem, bringing out the fact that God never ceases to watch over His people. Discuss God's immutability, or changelessness.

For part C, students are to make a simple motto of the poem. You could make photocopies to pass out or tell your students to copy it by hand. Have them illustrate the poem appropriately or make an attractive border. Glue onto construction paper and laminate.

Fifth Reader Workbook

 # 58. The Mother Teal and the Overland Route

This story is an excellent illustration of God's marvelous care for His creation. If God cares about baby teals like the ones in this story, we know He will take care of us.

A. Defining for Comprehension

Part I

h	1. sedge	a.	Having blotches or streaks of various colors.
e	2. pulsatory	b.	Soft, velvety cloth.
c	3. abounded	c.	Contained an abundance.
n	4. latter	d.	Dangerous; hazardous.
m	5. ominous	e.	Throbbing with life.
k	6. devotion	f.	Dwelling place.
g	7. drought	g.	Long period without rain.
d	8. perilous	h.	Marshland grass.
a	9. mottled	i.	That which feeds; food.
b	10. plush	j.	Compelling; demanding.
j	11. enforcing	k.	Strong affection and commitment.
l	12. sustained	l.	Kept alive.
i	13. nourishment	m.	Foretelling danger; threatening.
f	14. abode	n.	Near the end (of something).

Parts II and III

q	15. plaintively	o.	Group moving in an orderly way.
s	16. ventured	p.	Hung above; lingered over.
t	17. marshaled	q.	Woefully; sorrowfully.
o	18. procession	r.	Sprang upward; took off.
r	19. launched	s.	Dared to go.
p	20. hovered	t.	Arranged in order.

140

Lesson 58

To the Teacher

This story gives an excellent picture of God's marvelous care for His creation. As the students read, have them find all the things they can that God used to protect the little ducklings, such as the brush, the kingbird, and the man.

Note also the descriptive language used in the story. Instead of simply referring to them as eggs, the author used the expressions "china tombs" and "treasures of the teal," which portray the eggs as very precious. If the students imagine themselves to be as small as the downlings, they can better visualize such phrases as "bamboo forest" and "deep-worn, endless canyons."

Who made the "ominous crackling in the thick willows" and disturbed the mother teal's nest? Who was the "unseen power" that frightened away the fox? Who was the "heartless monster" that lifted the babies from the ruts? Explain that it was the author, and that he was God's means of protecting the babies.

Just as the author's good intentions were misunderstood by the mother teal, so we often misunderstand God in His dealings with us. His purposes are for our good, just as the author's purposes were for the good of the teals. Why did the mother teal fear him? ("His race had persecuted hers too long.") Of course, she could not know that the author wanted to help her.

You may choose to divide this lesson over two days

Use the following words to complete the sentences below.

askew   engulfed   strait
thwarted   direst   persecuted

21. The rain ___thwarted___ the farmer's plan to bale hay.

22. The thirsty people's ___direst___ need was water.

23. We were in a ___strait___ when two tires went flat at the same time.

24. Our travel plans went ___askew___ because of the flat tires.

25. The car was ___engulfed___ by a fog so thick that Father could not see the road.

26. The Christians were victorious even though they were ___persecuted___.

B. Reading for Comprehension

27. What do you think may have happened to the mother teal's mate? _____
    He was probably eaten by a fox or some other predator.

28. For what two reasons did the mother teal cover her eggs with a "foster mother" when she left the nest? (Hint: Think about temperature and enemies.)
    She covered the eggs to keep them warm and to hide them from enemies.

29. The first part of the story uses descriptive language when it calls the eggs "little china tombs." From the paragraph that has this expression, copy three descriptive phrases for the little downlings just after they hatched.
    little balls of mottled down, cushions of yellow plush, little golden caskets with
    jewel eyes

30. Did the ducklings need to have food immediately after they hatched? Explain your answer.
    No. They could live for a little while on the nourishment from the eggs.

31. What does the story mean when it refers to the marsh hawk's "crew of young marauders"?
    It means the young in the marsh hawk's nest.

32. Why did the kingbird attack the marsh hawk? _____
    The hawk flew over the kingbird's territory.

141

since it is a longer selection. You may want to copy and enlarge the drawing on page 240, and pass it out for the students to color.

Discussion Starters

1. Who made the crackling in the willows and disturbed the nest? (the author)
2. What was the bamboo forest? (tall stalks of grass)
3. What were the deep-worn, endless canyons? (wheel ruts)
4. Who lifted the babies from the ruts? (the author)
5. Name at least five animals that would hurt the babies. (harrier [marsh hawk], falcon, hawk, fox, weasel, coyote, snake)
6. How did the mother teal protect her family from the marsh hawk when it came the second time? (She used her feet and wings to dash water all over the hawk.)

Fifth Reader Workbook

33. In what two ways was the man a silent deliverer of the baby teals?_____

   by scaring away the fox and by helping the ducklings out of the wheel ruts

   _____

34. The mother teal tried to lure the man away from her young by pretending to be hurt. In what other story of this reader did a mother animal try to lure a man away?

   "The Fox Den"

C. Writing for Comprehension

35. Fill in the missing points in the following outline of this story.

   a.   The baby teals hatch.

   b.   The mother teal and her brood begin the journey to the pond.

   c.   A marsh hawk captures one duckling.

   d.   A fox approaches but flees when he senses that a man is near.

   e.   The ducklings become trapped in the wheel ruts.

   f.   A man rescues the ducklings from the ruts.

   g.   The marsh hawk attacks and is repelled again and again.

   h.   The captured duckling rejoins the others.

36. How did the drought increase danger for the mother teal and her young?_____

   It dried up the nearby pond and forced the teals to travel half a mile to another

   pond.

37. The last sentence of Part I says, "The countless living things about were either foes or neutral." Explain what this means.

   The surrounding creatures either were dangerous enemies or they ignored the

   mother teal. (None of them would help her.)

   _____

59. A Child of God

The young man in this story was given an offer similar to the one Moses received. Both could have become the son of an earthly king, but both chose to be a child of God. Both had to suffer, but God blessed them both for their wise choices.

A. Defining for Comprehension

Write the letter of the matching definition before each word.

_e_	1. unprecedented	a.	Shine forth; glow
_o_	2. resolutely	b.	Onlookers; watchers
_j_	3. station	c.	Opposition; defiance
_l_	4. perimeter	d.	Hate; loathe; despise
_c_	5. resistance	e.	Having never happened before
_h_	6. purge	f.	Unable to speak; mute
_n_	7. blasphemy	g.	Extreme distress; harshness
_b_	8. spectators	h.	Purify; cleanse
_k_	9. twinge	i.	Hardly noticeable; almost invisible
_g_	10. severity	j.	Place in position; post
_a_	11. radiate	k.	Sharp mental pain; pang
_i_	12. imperceptible	l.	Outer edge; border
_p_	13. frenzied	m.	Manner of carrying oneself; pose
_d_	14. abhor	n.	Disrespect toward God or sacred things
_m_	15. bearing	o.	With firm determination
_f_	16. dumb	p.	Wildly excited; extremely agitated

B. Reading for Comprehension

17. Diocletian had two main reasons for persecuting the Christians. One was that they refused to bow to him and the Roman gods. His other reason was actually based on a falsehood. What was the other reason?

    He blamed the Christians for planning to overthrow the government.

18. The story speaks of Diocletian shaking his fist, pounding the arms of his throne, and shouting. This shows him to be a fierce, violent man. Now read the paragraph that begins with "The prisoners' clothing hung in tatters." Find three words in the last sentence of that paragraph, which contrast the calmness of the Christians to the agitation of the emperor.

    tranquility, acceptance, peace

143

Lesson 59

To the Teacher

Before having the students read this story orally, give them some background information on the Roman Empire and the persecution of the early Christians. Explain that the Christians were suspected of disloyalty to the empire because they refused to worship the emperor.

The story gives a vivid picture of the emperor's character. Ask the pupils to find some words that suggest what mood the emperor was in. Then have them verify from the story such character traits as impatience, determination, and impulsiveness. Contrast the description of the emperor with that of the Christians, which includes words such as *radiate*, *tranquillity*, *acceptance*, and *peace*.

Compare Pancratius's opportunities with those of Moses. Both could have been sons of the king, but both refused, "choosing rather to suffer affliction with the people of God, than to enjoy the pleasures of sin for a season."

Discuss the principles of nonresistance as taught by Christ in Matthew 5:39–44 and as practiced by these Christians. What made it possible for them to face death with a song on their lips? Point out that the last paragraph is an appropriate ending to the story. Regardless of how hard the Roman emperors struggled against Christianity in trying to preserve their empire, it still crumbled. But the kingdom of our Lord endures to this day and will continue throughout eternity.

Fifth Reader Workbook

19. Why did Diocletian think that Pancratius would be willing to become his son? _____
    He thought surely Pancratius would rather become the emperor's son than suffer
    as a Christian.
    _____

20. Why did Pancratius refuse to become the emperor's son? _____
    Becoming the emperor's son included worshiping heathen gods, and Pancratius
    was determined to worship God alone.
    _____

21. Look in the middle part of Hebrews 11, and write the numbers of three verses that tell how Moses made the same choice that Pancratius made. __verses 24–26__

C. Writing for Comprehension

22. A good reader is someone who both understands and thinks about what he reads. If we cannot understand a word in a story, we need to use a dictionary to make sure we grasp what the author is saying.

    A good reader prefers **worthwhile stories** that contain information about profitable subjects. Such stories increase our understanding of truth and are always based on truth. This does not mean the stories must be true, but it does mean that they teach valuable lessons which agree with what the Bible teaches.

    Write a paragraph explaining why "A Child of God" is a worthwhile story. Think about the truths that the story teaches.

    (Sample points to be included in the paragraph.)
    It is based on truth and deals with a worthwhile subject (loyalty to God).
    It describes the suffering that Christians are willing to endure for Christ.
    It shows that the works of men pass away, but the Word of God endures forever.
    It agrees with the Bible on the principle of nonresistance and the power of faith.
    It is inspiring and worthwhile reading.

144

Literary concept in this lesson:

Worthwhile stories (Discuss exercise 22 in class.)

Discussion Starters

1. What doubts did Diocletian have about the idea of adopting Pancratius? (He wondered what his senators and generals would think. He realized that Pancratius might refuse.)

2. Describe how the group of prisoners looked. (Their clothes were tattered. They had been beaten. Many were limping. The strong supported the weak. A sense of peace radiated from them.)

3. The old man was "looking squarely at Diocletian" as he spoke. What is meant by this expression? (He was looking directly at Diocletian.)

4. Why do you suppose the emperor hated to hear the Christians singing? (It probably made him feel guilty.)

5. Which sentence in the story contains the title of the story? ("I would rather die as a child of God than live as your son.")

60. The Good Samaritan

From this story that Jesus told, we learn that being a good neighbor is much more than getting along well with people who live close to us. Rather, it means helping someone in need, regardless of who the person is. Being a Good Samaritan often involves a sacrifice on our part as we help another person. Notice that the Samaritan in this story paid two days' wages for the continued care of the injured man after he had provided for his immediate needs.

Anyone who is a Good Samaritan must love other people. If we fail to love, we are not likely to go out of our way to help someone. This was obviously true of the priest and the Levite in this story. The Bible tells us that it is more blessed to give than to receive. Being a Good Samaritan brings rich rewards.

For this last composition assignment, write a story showing how one person was a good neighbor to another. You may be able to think of something that actually happened, or you may use your imagination and write a true-to-life story. Perhaps you can combine the two by enlarging on an actual happening. Whichever you choose, keep the central theme in mind: A good neighbor is someone who is willing to help another person in need.

Write an outline of your story plot before you begin. Also review the Keys to Good Writing in Lesson 12. Write your story on other paper. (Grade students' work for content and grammar. Be sure the story sticks to the theme and is true to life.

Review for Test 10

1. Be sure you know the meanings of the vocabulary words in Lessons 55–60.

2. Be sure you know the qualities of a worthwhile story and a good reader. See Lesson 59.

3. Be sure you know what these terms mean. They are all from earlier lessons.

    mood words (Lesson 16)

    plot (Lesson 25)

    outline (Lesson 46)

145

Lesson 60

To the Teacher

Discuss this parable with the students. Point out that a Christian's love for God is revealed as he expresses the love of God toward his neighbors (fellow men). A Christian cannot love God without also loving his neighbor (1 John 3:11–18). Furthermore, "love worketh no ill to his neighbour" (Romans 13:8–10).

Encourage the students to do their best as they write this final composition for reading class.

A Time to Plant (Lessons 1–6)   **Test 1**

Name: _____

Date: _____   **Score:** _____

A. Concentrate carefully as your teacher reads several paragraphs orally. Then on the lines below, answer the questions that your teacher asks about the paragraphs. (Teacher: See paragraphs following test.)

1. Ireland _____

2. Ned _____

3. 15 years _____

4. make a basket _____

B. Write the letter of the matching definition before each word.

  b   5. infinite

  i   6. relentless

  g   7. gait

  f   8. medley

  h   9. fare

  c   10. fragile

  e   11. persuade

  d   12. gorged

  a   13. eerie

a. Weird; unnatural; frightening.

b. Boundless or eternal.

c. Delicate; easily broken.

d. Ate greedily.

e. Convince; make someone believe.

f. Confused mixture; jumble.

g. Manner of walking or running.

h. Money charged for a ride.

i. Without slackening; persistent.

14. Use the word **figure** as a noun in a sentence of your own. (Sample answer.)

    A lone figure strode along the beach. _____

C. Write the missing words in the long blanks after the sentences.

15. The setting of a story is the ___ and ___ in which the story occurs. (Either order.)

    place, time _____

16. A good ___ is a picture or diagram that makes writing clearer by helping the reader to "see" something. __illustration__

17. The most important truth or lesson in a story is the ___ ___ of the story.
    __main idea__

18. We are ___ ___ ___ when we learn what a new word means by the way it is used in a sentence.
    __defining from context__

19. The ___ ___ is the author's most important reason for writing a story.
    __writer's purpose__

D. Write whether each statement is true (T) or false (F).

__T__ 20. The story "To Market" story took place in the Philippines.

__T__ 21. Sharing makes us happy.

__F__ 22. The boy in "The Second Mile" carried a pack for a Greek soldier.

__F__ 23. A barometer is an instrument to measure changes in water pressure.

__T__ 24. The last syllable of **mischief** rhymes with **whiff.**

__F__ 25. The Bible tells us to return evil for good.

Teacher: Read the following paragraphs slowly and clearly one time. Then have the students answer the questions below.

Many years ago, in the county of Cavon, Ireland, there lived an elderly lady who was known far and wide for her deeds of kindness. Mrs. Farnham was her name, and she had enough money that she could have lived in pleasure. But knowing that "she that liveth in pleasure is dead while she liveth," she had chosen rather to live a plain and quiet life.

Near this lady lived a family so poor that they were considered hopeless by many. Their oldest boy, fifteen-year-old Ned, met Mrs. Farnham one morning near her house and begged for something for his family to eat. Mrs. Farnham stopped, and looking at him, she said, "My boy, I would like you to do something to earn your bread. Make me a basket. As soon as you have finished, bring it to me and I will pay you well for it."

Questions:

1. In what country did the story take place?

2. What was the boy's name?

3. How old was the boy?

4. What did the lady want the boy to do?

A Time to Plant (Lessons 7–12)   Test 2

Name: _____

Date: _____   Score: _____

A. *Concentrate carefully as your teacher reads a paragraph orally. Then on the lines below, answer the questions that your teacher asks about the paragraph.* (Teacher: See paragraph following test.)

1. __twelve_____

2. __hummingbird_____

3. __swallows_____

4. __plowing_____

B. *Cross out the word in each group that does not fit with the others.*

5. larva, adult, pupa, ~~honey~~

6. scheme, hoax, plot, ~~specimen~~

7. vexed, brooded, ~~enthusiastic~~, remorse

8. guidance, counsel, ~~reflect~~, help

9. companionable, ~~irritable~~, considerate, understanding

C. *Write the correct word or phrase for each description.*

10. A comparison such as a simile or metaphor, which helps us get a clearer understanding of something. __figure of speech_____

11. A composition that teaches a lesson by telling about an event in the life of one or more characters.

    __story_____

12. A composition that presents facts or opinions about a subject, usually without characters.

    __essay_____

D. *Write whether each sentence contains a simile (S) or a metaphor (M).*

__M__ 13. The sky was a gray blanket.

__S__ 14. The grass was as soft as a carpet.

__S__ 15. The old truck rattled like a tin can.

E. Write four of the seven Keys to Good Writing.   (Any four keys. Three keys are abbreviated.)

Think about what you want to say before you begin writing.	Be concise.
Do not wander from your theme or main idea.	Be precise.
Work neatly. Check your spelling and punctuation.	Make sense.
Rewrite your work until you are satisfied that you have done your best.	

Paragraph to read orally for Part A:

Twelve-year-old Stewart squirmed restlessly in his chair. Distracted by the hummingbird, he turned to look out the window. Oh, how nice it looked outside! Swallows were darting about. A little green grass was beginning to appear, and the water sparkled in the small creek that bordered the schoolyard. Beyond the creek, neighbor Anderson was plowing. "Sure wish I was on that tractor instead of in this schoolroom," Stewart thought to himself.

Questions:

1. How old was Stewart?

2. What kind of bird distracted Stewart?

3. What other birds were darting about?

4. What was neighbor Anderson doing?

🌱 A Time to Plant (Lessons 13–18)   Test 3

Name: _____

Date: _____   **Score:** _____

A. Concentrate carefully as your teacher reads several paragraphs orally. Then on the lines below, answer the questions that your teacher asks about the paragraphs.   (Teacher: See paragraphs following test.)

1. one or two months

2. a pocketknife

3. in the dense brush bordering the schoolyard

4. by riding a horse

5. one of his classmates

6. tied to the fence (on the other side of the building)

B. Cross out the word in each group that does not fit with the rest.

7. palm, mango, carabao, ~~Inuit~~

8. sad, depressed, ~~tantalizing~~, melancholy

9. salesmen, vendors, ~~array~~, peddlers

10. ~~adder~~, fowler, bird, feather

11. summoned, called, requested, ~~extinguished~~

12. anxious, ~~eager~~, worried, uneasy

13. ~~circle~~, semicircle, half circle, half moon

C. Write whether each word suggests a feeling of calmness (C) or excitement (E).

_C_ 14. breeze   _E_ 17. startled

_E_ 15. lunging   _C_ 18. drifted

_E_ 16. alarm   _C_ 19. tranquil

D. Use these terms to fill in the blanks. You will not use them all.

fiction   main character   mood words
prose   opening paragraph   parallel lines

20. In "Danger in the Wind," Stewart is the main character

21. A composition that is not written as a poem is called _____ prose _____

22. A story about imaginary characters and events is called _____ fiction _____

23. To make a person want to read on, a story should have a good ___ opening paragraph _____

24. In Bible poetry, phrases with "rhyming thoughts" are called _____ parallel lines _____

Paragraph for Part A:

Armando was puzzled. Did the teacher think he had taken Rodrigo's money? Why, it had been all of a month or two since he had picked up anything that was not his. Then a truly frightening thought came to him. What if Rodrigo should claim to recognize a particular coin he had? What if he could not make them believe him? They must not take his money away from him. He had almost felt that pocketknife in his hand, and now he could not bear to lose it.

Armando thought rapidly. Neither Brother Montealegre nor Rodrigo was yet in sight. Desperately, Armando bolted for the door. Once outside, he ran swiftly across the schoolyard toward a cover of bushes and trees. Just as he reached the edge of the cover, he heard a classmate's shout, "Armando's running away!"

He kept running, then threw himself face down in an area of dense brush. He was sure the teacher would not find him there, even if he did leave classwork to search for him—an unlikely possibility.

Armando had ridden a horse to school that morning. Now he thought, "If only I could get to my horse, I could get away faster." But he had left the horse tied to the fence on the other side of the building. Did he dare risk being seen? Moving slowly and always keeping low, he crept into the high pasture bordering the schoolhouse. Once he raised his head cautiously to peer at the building and saw Brother Montealegre on the porch, scanning the area carefully. He could hear him calling his name. It was then that Armando began to mutter his feelings against adults.

Questions:

1. How long had it been since Armando had last stolen something?

2. What did he want to buy with his money?

3. Where did Armando hide?

4. How had Armando gotten to school?

5. Who shouted, "Armando's running away!"

6. Where had Armando left his horse?

A Time to Plant (Lessons 19–24)   **Test 4**

Name: _____

Date: _____   **Score:** _____

A. How well did you concentrate in Lesson 22? Circle the letter of the correct answer.

1. About how much did the beaver weigh?

    a. six pounds   b. sixteen pounds   (c.) sixty pounds

2. What was the main reason for the beavers' canal from the felling area to the main pond?

    a. convenience   (b.) safety   c. recreation

3. Can a beaver control the direction that a tree will fall?

    a. always   (b.) never   c. sometimes

4. When do a beaver's teeth stop growing?

    a. in old age   b. in infancy   (c.) not as long as the beaver lives

5. At what level was the beaver family's living quarters located?

    (a.) above the surface of the pond

    b. just below the surface of the pond

    c. at the bottom of the pond

6. Where did the beavers store their supply of food for winter?

    a. at the felling area   (b.) under the water   c. in the canal

B. Cross out the word in each group that does not fit with the others.

7. force, compel, ~~urchin~~, constrain

8. clumsy, ~~sporadic~~, awkward, cumbersome

9. ~~rueful~~, drastic, extreme, severe

10. garbage, debris, ~~unperturbed~~, rubbish

11. thoroughfare, street, ~~city~~, road

12. ~~familiar~~, infinite, boundless, unlimited

13. skiff, boat, canoe, ~~poised~~

C. Answer these questions.

14. By one pattern in poetry, the last words of some lines have endings that sound alike. What do we call this pattern? __rhyme__

15. By another pattern in poetry, words have a regular arrangement of accented and unaccented syllables. What do we call this pattern? __rhythm__

16. What does the narrator of a story do? _____

    __The narrator tells the story.__

17. What is one way to capture the reader's attention in the opening paragraph?

    (Either answer.)

    __by raising questions in the reader's mind;__

    __by suggesting that something exciting is about to happen__

18. What do we do when we visualize? _____

    __We see in our minds what is happening in the story.__

19. What are we doing when we use other books to check the accuracy of what we read?

    __We are verifying.__

20. These sentences are about main ideas. Write whether each one is true **(T)** or false **(F).**

    __F__   a. In "A Night on the Mississippi," the boys ran into many dangers.

    __T__   b. Smiles grow very rapidly.

    __T__   c. Beavers need to work together to survive.

    __F__   d. Being brave means doing things that people notice.

    __T__   e. To solve misunderstandings, we need to look at other people's view of things.

A Time to Plant (Lessons 25–30)   Test 5

Name: _____

Date: _____   **Score:** _____

A. Answer these questions to show how well you concentrated in Lessons 25–30.

1. What was the probable reason for Judge Louis's death?

   It was probably God's judgment for persecuting innocent Christians.

2. a. What two things are compared to each other in the poem about the blacksmith?

   an anvil and the Bible

   b. What truth does this comparison teach?

   God's Word will always endure, no matter what people do to oppose it.

3. What is the main activity in the story "Salmon Days"?

   The family was catching salmon for their winter supply of food.

4. What lesson can we learn from the story about Susan's temptation?   (Sample answers.)

   honesty; admitting our mistakes; doing what our parents teach us

B. Write whether each pair of words is a synonym (S) or an antonym (A).

A 5. vigilant, drowsy

A 6. abruptly, gradually

A 7. commotion, stillness

S 8. extract, remove

A 9. descend, ascend

S 10. impatient, impulsive

S 11. scornful, disrespectful

A 12. improvements, desolations

S 13. refuge, protection

A 14. impractical, workable

A 15. prisoner, bailiff

C. *Write the correct words in the blanks below. You will not use all the words.*

        plot   suspense
        research   metaphor
        taking notes   main idea

16. When we use reference books to find more information, we are doing __research__

17. The pattern of events in a story is called the _____ __plot__

18. Writing down the main ideas that a speaker gives is called _____ __taking notes__

19. The reader's uncertainty about the outcome of a story is called _____ __suspense__

D. *Write* **X** *before each sentence that contains a figure of speech. If it does, write* **simile** *or* **metaphor** *after the sentence.*

_____ 20. A desperate effort at the oars told how willing the men were to obey. _____

_**X**_ 21. They draped the fish carefully over slender poles, like towels on a washline. ___simile___

_____ 22. Needless to say, the brethren inside the house had heard the commotion and hurried out the back door. _____

_**X**_ 23. And so, I thought, the anvil of God's Word

        For ages skeptics' blows have beat upon. __metaphor__

A Time to Plant (Lessons 31–36)   Test 6

Name: _____

Date: _____   **Score:** _____

A. Read the following paragraph from "Mary's Bible," and list eight details that it contains.

It was now afternoon, and the sun was hot. The way stretched along a dusty road, and Mary felt her bare feet grow sore and tired as she plodded on. Once she saw a woman standing in a cottage garden, who looked kindly over the hedge at her.

(Any eight of the following details. Allow ten minutes for this exercise.)	
It was afternoon.	The sun was hot.
Mary was walking down the road.	The road was dusty.
Mary's feet were bare.	Her feet grew sore and tired.
She saw a woman.	
The woman was standing in a cottage garden.	
The woman looked kindly at Mary.	
There was a hedge between Mary and the woman.	

*B. Write **T** (true) or **F** (false) to tell whether each word in bold print is defined correctly.*

   T   1. **erect**—upright; vertical

   F   2. **carcasses**—bodies of live animals

   T   3. **havoc**—confusion; disorder

   T   4. **abundant**—bountiful; plenteous

   T   5. **seldom**—not often; rarely

   F   6. **response**—leaving; deserting

   T   7. **disheartened**—discouraged; depressed

   T   8. **proverb**—wise saying

   F   9. **consistent**—pretended; imaginary

   F   10. **overwhelming**—reverent; respectful

   F   11. **extensive**—genuine; sincere

_T_ 12. **pagan**—heathen; idolatrous

_F_ 13. **wary**—sluggish; lazy

_T_ 14. **inhospitable**—providing no shelter or comfort

_T_ 15. **rent**—a tear as in cloth

C. *Choose from the following words to fill in the blanks below.*

detail, metaphor, parable, simile, summary, verifying, visualizing

16. An earthly story with a heavenly meaning is a ___parable_____

17. We are ___verifying___ information when we check facts by using an encyclopedia.

18. A figurative comparison that uses **like** or **as** is a ___simile_____

19. When we form a mental picture of what we read, we are ___visualizing_____

20. A paragraph that sums up the main details of a story is called a ___summary_____

D. *Match the titles of the last six lessons to their main ideas.*

a. A Mother Bear Story   d. Mary's Bible

b. John Maynard   e. The Oil or the Book

c. Perseverance   f. The Rich Fool

_c_ 21. We finish large tasks by patiently sticking to the small details.

_e_ 22. Reading is a great help in serving God.

_a_ 23. We can learn interesting facts by studying things in nature.

_f_ 24. God is displeased with selfishness; He wants us to share.

_b_ 25. Difficulties in life reveal a person's true character.

_d_ 26. The Bible is a great treasure that we should love.

A Time to Plant (Lessons 37–42)   **Test 7**

Name: _____

Date: _____   **Score:** _____

A. Concentrate carefully as your teacher reads two paragraphs from "A Night on the Mississippi."
Then on the lines below, answer the questions that your teacher asks about the paragraphs.

(Teacher: See paragraphs following test.)

1.   a dull, dark line _____

2.   (Any two.) birds twittering, raftmen's voices, a sweep creaking _____

3.   in the morning (at dawn) _____

4.   mist _____

B. Write **T** *(true) or* **F** *(false) to tell whether each word in bold print is defined correctly.*

T   5. **wretched**—miserable; unhappy

T   6. **similar**—resembling; like

T   7. **bliss**—great happiness; joy

F   8. **remote**—close at hand; nearby

F   9. **anguish**—wrath; anger

T   10. **spacious**—roomy

F   11. **reluctant**—willing; eager

T   12. **ascends**—goes up

F   13. **colloquy**—lonely thoughts

T   14. **picturesque**—beautiful

T   15. **tawdry**—of poor quality

F   16. **drones**—female bees

C. Write the answers.

17. Descriptive writing may form pictures in our minds. This is called __imagery__

18. A biography is ___the story (account) of a person's life___

19. Which of these stories is a biography? Circle the correct letter.

    (a.) The Brickfields of Bristol (main character: John Wesley)

    b. The Lost Boy (main character: Charles)

    c. The Beautiful Home (main character: Lois)

20. The author of "The Beautiful Home" wrote this story to show that we should not judge by outward appearance. Such a reason is called the ___writer's purpose___

21. Use the symbols / and ∪ to mark the rhythm pattern of the following line of poetry.

    /   ∪   / ∪   /   ∪   /
    School can be a hap-py place.

22. The _____rhyme_____ pattern of a poem is the pattern in which the last words of some lines have endings that sound alike.

Paragraphs for Part A:

(Read the following passage twice, slowly and clearly. Tell the students to concentrate on the sights and sounds that the passage portrays.)

First, looking away over the water, I could see a dull, dark line. That was the wooded shore of the other side. The birds twittered softly in the trees close at hand. Then there came a faint, pale light in the sky; then the river softened from black to gray; and far out I could see small, dusky spots drifting along.

Once there was a long, black line and I knew it to be a raft like ours, only much larger and heavier. I faintly heard the raftmen's voices and a sweep creaking. Then a streak on the water showed where a snag lay hidden beneath, ready to catch and snap some unwary oar. By and by the mist drew itself up from the river in fleecy twists and swirls, the east began to redden, a breeze sprang up, and lines of smoke rose from the hillside behind us. At last the full day broke and everything smiled in the sunshine.

Questions:

1. What was the first thing the narrator saw as he looked over the water?

2. What were two sounds that the narrator heard?

3. At what time of day does this account take place?

4. What "drew itself up from the river in fleecy twists and swirls"?

A Time to Plant (Lessons 43–48)   Test 8

Name: _____

Date: _____   **Score:** _____

A. Write whether the two words in each pair are synonyms (S) or antonyms (A).

  A   1. idle, working

  A   2. wrought, slept

  S   3. borne, endured

  S   4. resolved, determined

  A   5. charitable, malicious

  S   6. encountered, faced

  S   7. anticipation, expectation

  S   8. perplexed, baffled

  A   9. native, foreign

  S 10. flexible, pliant

  S 11. compensate, offset

  S 12. petroleum, oil

  S 13. procedure, method

  A 14. graciously, bitterly

  S 15. junction, meeting

B. Write the answers.

16. The _____outline_____ of a composition is a list of the main ideas or events in the order they appear.

17. The _____theme_____ of a composition is the same as its main idea.

18. A _____parable_____ is an earthly story with a heavenly meaning.

19. What is the difference between a story that is fiction and one that is nonfiction?

    ____If it is fiction, it has imaginary characters and events._____

    ____If it is nonfiction, the events actually happened._____.

20. Here are the points for an outline of "The Laborers in the Vineyard." Number them in the correct order.

    __2__ a. The laborers agreed to work all day for one penny.

    __6__ b. The householder said that he was allowed to pay all the workers the same if he wished.

    __3__ c. The householder hired laborers at the third, sixth, ninth, and eleventh hours.

    __1__ d. A householder went to the market one morning to hire laborers for his vineyard.

    __5__ e. The laborers who had worked all day complained that the householder was unfair.

    __4__ f. The steward called the laborers and paid them each one penny.

A Time to Plant (Lessons 49–54)   Test 9

Name: _____

Date: _____ •_____   **Score:** _____

A. Read the following paragraphs, and answer the questions below.

The emperor Diocletian slouched among the purple velvet cushions of the imperial throne, chewing impatiently on a fingernail. His eyes darted restlessly over the noisy crowd gathering in his Hall of Justice.

Today he would condemn another group of those traitorous Christians who refused to bow to his supreme power. He was determined to put an end to their efforts to undermine his leadership!

For a moment, the scowl left his face. The youth, Pancratius, who had stood before him yesterday, would be brought forward again.

1. Diocletian was not a king. What kind of ruler was he? __emperor_____

2. What color were the cushions on his throne? __purple_____

3. What are two words that suggest Diocletian's mood? __(Sample answers.)_____

   __slouched, impatiently, restlessly, determined_____

4. What kind of people were to be brought before him? __Christians_____

5. What was the name of the youth who would stand before Diocletian? __Pancratius_____

B. Cross out the word in each group that does not fit.

6. turbulent, raging, unsettled, ~~sauntering~~

7. strikes, ~~puffs~~, pelts, buffets

8. solitude, loneliness, ~~security~~, secluded

9. action, gesture, motion, ~~folly~~

10. scurried, ~~immense~~, clamber, descending

11. ~~torrents~~, thoughts, musings, meditations

C. Write the correct words.

12. A story title should hint at the main idea, but it should not give away the __outcome (ending)__

13. A paragraph that sums up the most important details of a story is called a __summary__

D. Underline the rhyming words in this poem. Use / and ⌣ to mark the rhythm pattern.

⌣   /   ⌣   / ⌣ / ⌣ /
Sleep sweet with-in this qui-et room,

⌣ /   ⌣   /   ⌣   /
O thou, who-e'er thou <u>art,</u>

⌣ / ⌣   /   ⌣ / ⌣   /
And let no mourn-ful yes-ter-days

⌣ / ⌣   /   ⌣   /
Dis-turb thy peace-ful <u>heart.</u>

A Time to Plant (Lessons 55–60)   Test 10

Name: _____

Date: _____   Score: _____

A. Write **yes** *or* **no** *before each word to tell whether it would help to create a mood in a story.*

   yes   1. tranquil

   no   2. car

   yes   3. misty

   no   4. jug

   no   5. reply

   yes   6. rage

   yes   7. suddenly

   yes   8. whisper

   no   9. paper

   yes 10. silent

B. Write the letter of the matching definition before each word.

   d   11. auditorium   a. Fellow worker.

   h   12. inquired   b. Defeated; frustrated.

   e   13. modification   c. Completely; totally.

   a   14. colleague   d. Large room where listeners sit.

   f   15. drought   e. Change; adjustment.

   j   16. engulfed   f. Long dry spell.

   b   17. thwarted   g. Purify; cleanse.

   g   18. purge   h. Asked; questioned.

   c   19. utterly   i. Hate; loathe; despise.

   i   20. abhor   j. Enclosed completely; swallowed up.

C. Write or choose the correct answers.

21. The ___outline___ of a story is a list of the main events in the order they happened.

22. The ___plot___ of a story is the pattern of events in the story.

23. What are two qualities of a worthwhile story?   (Sample answers.)

    It is about a worthwhile subject.   It is based on truth.

    It teaches a good lesson.   It agrees with the Bible.

24. "John ran like a deer" contains a (<u>simile</u>, metaphor).

25. When you (<u>summarize</u>, verify) a story, you make a list of the main points.

26. A (story plot, <u>biography</u>) is the story of a person's life.

27. If a story is (fiction, <u>nonfiction</u>), the story is true.

D. Tell one lesson that a reader can learn from each of these stories. The words in parentheses give a hint of what the story was about.   (Sample answers given.)

28. "Language Without *Love*" (missionary, Africa, translation) _____

    perseverance, dedication

29. "Brother David's Song" (Jill, singing) _____

    respect for old people, patience

30. "A Child of God" (persecution, Pancratius) _____

    faithfulness in persecution, nonresistance